The
ROAR
of
SILENCE

Cover Art: *Star of the Hero* by Nicholas Roerich. Reproduced with permission of Nicholas Roerich Museum, 319 W. 107th St., New York, NY.

Interior Art: Illustrations opposite the meditations are from *Thought Forms* by Annie Besant and C. W. Leadbeater. Published by the Theosophical Publishing House, Wheaton, Illinois.

The ROAR of SILENCE

*Healing Powers of
Breath, Tone & Music*

Don G. Campbell

This publication is made possible with
the assistance of the Kern Foundation

The Theosophical Publishing House
Wheaton, Ill. U.S.A.
Madras, India/London, England

For information regarding permission to quote from this
book please write to:

The Theosophical Publishing House
306 West Geneva Road
Wheaton, IL 60187

A publication of the Theosophical Publishing House, a
department of the Theosophical Society in America.

Library of Congress Cataloging-in-Publication Data

Campbell, Don G.
    The roar of silence : healing powers of breath, tone &
music / Don G. Campbell. — 1st ed.
        p.   cm. — (Quest books)
    Bibliography: p.
    Discography: p.
    ISBN 0-8356-0645-7 : $9.95
    1. Sound—Therapeutic use.   2. Vibration—Therapeutic
use.   3. Psychoacoustics.   4. Healing.   I. Title.
RZ999.C195   1989
615.8'3—dc20   89-40173
                                                        CIP

Printed in the United States of America

*To the wounded listener and sleeping musician
in each of us*

Contents

Foreword by Jean Houston   ix
Acknowledgments   xi
Prelude: My Journey into Toning   1
How to Use this Book   15

Chapter 1
Meditation: Sacred Breath, Sacred Life   19
Awakening Vibratory Awareness   20
Exercise: Toning the Body   25

Chapter 2
Meditation: The Pulse of Life   29
The Wounded Listener:
Balancing Inner and Outer Sound   30
Exercise: Healing the Listener   38

Chapter 3
Meditation: The All in Every Sound   43
The Energy Beneath Sound:
Sound Waves and the Brain   44
Exercise: Exploring the Depths of Memory   52

Chapter 4
Meditation: Aaah-Haah   57
Toning, Chanting and Singing   58
Exercise: Awakening the Sonic Spectrum   77

Chapter 5
Meditation: The Sound of Peace   81
Transformation through Sound:
Effects on Body, Mind and Spirit   82
Exercise: Exploring the Vibratory Centers   97

Chapter 6
Meditation: The Wings of Song   101
The Overtones of Health   103
Exercise: Making Overtones   114

Chapter 7
Meditation: The Ancient Future   119
The Sound of Light   121
Exercise: The Roar of Silence   128

Bibliography   129
Discography   132

Foreword
Jean Houston

The account by modern physicists of the way stars implode and explode, thus creating other star systems and the elements that, in our case at least, have gone into the evolution of life, thrills me for many reasons. But the primary theory that thrills me is the one they present of sound and sound vibration as the heart-mother of all being.

Helping the individual attune to that great universal sound and find the resonance within, enabling one to partake in the power of that sound, is something Don Campbell has been studying, reflecting upon and teaching with consummate skill for many years. Now at last, the essence of his teaching and thought is available through the meditations and discussion offered here.

This is a book to do and redo and listen to as one creates the great inner sounding which can help align us with the eternal sound emanating from the heart of the universe.

Acknowledgments

I am indebted to many of my associates and friends. They have taught me patience, awareness, and how to listen. Special gratitude goes to: Laurie Rugenstein, my assistant, who has truly developed the ear of deep listening for the powers within tone; Jonathan Goldman, director of the Sound Healers Association, who introduced me to the masters of sound within my own voice; Sharon Gillespie, who read the text and tested every dimension of the meditations and exercises; Marie Carmichael and the dozens of students and mentees at the Institute for Music, Health and Education and Naropa Institute, who helped me develop ways to teach the benefits of toning.

Very special thanks go to: Dr. Dee Joy Coulter, who has given me endless moments of "Ah Ha" with insights on consciousness, the brain, and my work with tone; Perry McKay, who has supported the research projects on sound and tone at the Institute for Music, Health and Education in Boulder, Colorado; Shirley Nicholson and William Metzger of the Theosophical Society, who encouraged me to write about my mesoteric studies; and The Venerable Tai Situ Rimpoche, who reminded me of what I had forgotten, that the transmission of love is simple.

Prelude:
My Journey into Toning

I have always known there are powers within music, sound, and light that are far more potent than the arts themselves. Yet the arts have carried that vibratory power to the depths of my soul. Nevertheless, years in conservatory study as a pianist and organist in Europe and America have yielded few clues for naming that transformation and healing power held within the structure of the sonic arts.

My inner quest through the history and performance of Western music was like walking through a giant labyrinth. I would get close to the source, a place nearly beyond thought, a place where spirit, soul, and body were in resonance. Then, with a small amount of inertia, I would somehow find myself facing another direction, heading away from that beloved space.

Working as a teacher, writer, composer, and healer, I continually oscillated between a fascinating world of dynamic research and a world of inner awareness that is unnamable. Months spent in isolation making elongated sounds with my voice and body contrasted sharply with the years of reading, lecturing, and traveling. The sensory stimulation necessary to awaken the brain to creative and joyous growth became a powerful contrast to the very core of awareness—that "pure

1

being," "silent awakening," and "beyond body and brain" state, clearly related by mystics, Zen masters, and Kabbalists. It took years of searching to find the keys to the healing power of sound.

I think my odyssey started when I was five. I can still hear the rhythm of the scratches on my 78 r.p.m. of Daffy Duck singing silly words to Brahms' "Hungarian Rhapsody." I can still feel the movements of my body as I gestured to "I'm a Little Tea Pot" in my Sunday school class. I can still hear the organ music when I first realized that someone served teeny tiny refreshments in itsy bitsy glasses with blah-blah crackers at church. I can still feel the hard gym floor and brown piece of paper that my little body rested on after lunch in kindergarten while Sister Mary Somebody played "The Laughing Phonograph." I pretended to lie still, pretended to be asleep, I was really dancing all over the ceiling, making faces at the teacher and the other students. I remember my first piano piece at age five when I used my favorite "pointing" fingers, but it wasn't nice to point. I can smell the furniture polish on our dining room table as I played "Dites Moi" from South Pacific and found real meaning in the words I did not have to think about. I still can hear the sounds of saws and hammers in my father's workshop, far too loud to be close to, but they made one long, long, long sound with their sharp, bright tones.

Everything was sight, sound, stimulation, and wiggling down information with sound. Every breath was a new dictionary of perception. Music was the pleasure, the purpose, the power that moved everything. Dad walked and whistled, Mom cooked, Mimi, my grandmother, rocked in her chair, Perfume, the cat, purred. It was all music. Everything was alive with a rhythm I knew nothing about, but knew intimately and thoroughly.

. . .Until Sister Mary Claude told me to sit down, be quiet and learn. I wondered what she thought I had been doing for the last five years. She told me to focus my eyes on a book at an awkward distance, sit in this hard, awful chair and be nice because I would be rewarded in heaven. But there in Sacred Heart Catholic school for thirty minutes a day, my Methodist ears were able to hear beautiful long, long tones and music. We had to stand on our knees so we could hear better and sing songs without words in God's secret language rather than in Texan English.

Then the musical forgetting began. There were long periods when the only music I heard was the songs in my head and feet. I learned the "clocking speel" part of the Toy Symphony. I learned the piano. I joined the church choir. I took clarinet. I knew Dad would buy me an electric organ if I would learn "Clair de lune," so I learned "Liebestraum" by mistake and got a Wurlitzer. I sang solo. I became assistant to the assistant drum major and at last learned all the harmonic minor scales. I had developed the habit of practicing music. I studied all the Italian words. Then, boom—it hit. Music was a full-time job. It only felt good when I got it right, and then it was more of a release. I still remembered how to listen; I could still dance inside, and slip the shackles of time and space. But I was hooked on knowing, naming, performing, and controlling music.

One evening at the end of eighth grade in San Antonio, Texas, my father said we would soon be moving to France. He had accepted a new job with the government. Suddenly I was in a Catholic country. There were rivers, grand towers, and a new form of intrigue, the Gothic cathedral. I was stunned to find something equal to music. And I was completely overwhelmed to find the music within long, long, long sounds that made me feel like crying. I was totally exalted by the music of the organ, the beauty of the choir. Though I missed the band, I missed my friends, I missed the familiar, I still loved this new air. I began to remember how to dance.

I cannot forget any detail of my fourth day in France. We were staying on the third floor of a small hotel in Fontainebleau with a perfect view of the chateau. A magnificent palace with gardens, cobblestone walkways, and horseshoe-shaped staircases. My father took me to the palace for an audition that would change my life. I walked into a mirrored room with an ornamented ceiling, crafted fireplaces, and wooden floors, to play a piano that seemed longer than our car. Seated behind a table in the room were people who were finely dressed and seemed very old. They had beautiful names: Nadia Boulanger, Jean Casadesus, and Annette Dieudonné. I played Grieg, Beethoven, and Bach pieces "by heart." The following day, my father received a letter inviting me to attend the Conservatory of Music for the next six weeks. I was thirteen years old.

I remember thinking how much fun it would be to take a class in piano pedagogy and learn how to use the three pedals. Soon Hindemith's *Elementary Training for Musicians* made me realize that I knew little about music. The rigor of reading a half-dozen clefs in three lines and taking four-part dictation soon began to create a pressure and tension like none I had ever known. Because I was the youngest student, my esteemed teachers showed patience, but I began to feel the weight of becoming a musician, that music was hard, hard work. I realized that my fingers could not move cleanly enough. Hours and hours of practice brought equal amounts of frustration and joy.

I recall sitting in the garden of the Fontainebleau palace near the statue of Diana one afternoon. No matter how hard I tried, I knew I could never be good enough. It was time to stop this music study; it was simply too difficult. But I was stuck. What else was there to do in life? Music was fresh, honest, beautiful, and made me feel wonderful. Nothing else called me to life except the beauty of art and architecture that I had just discovered. But I had no talent in those fields. I had made no friends. I first realized that music was the closest friend I had ever had, and now for the first time I was not good enough to be its friend. I could hear ten pianos playing in distant practice rooms and the organ playing Franck. I was sad because my intuitive dance had to slow down and sometimes stop so my fingers could learn technique and my brain could learn theory. But there was no choice. I had to live and learn music.

By the time I entered college, I was a fairly normal obsessed young musician. I loved the history, the theory, the ear training, and the study of Bach fugues on the organ. I enjoyed singing in massive choirs with hundreds of voices. Hearing Mahler, Berg and Buxtehude brought new music to my mind and heart. North Texas State University had a powerful jazz department, and I secretly admired the inner dancing that was happening in a nearby building. But I could not be distracted from the formal music education that would free me to be myself: a music teacher. To pass on the glories of sound to others. To introduce children to Fauré, Bach, and string quartets.

I finally knew so much about music that I had forgotten how to dance, how to feel and create tones. I was not a composer then; musical creativity had to come through interpretation and manners of presentation. I was qualified and gifted and graduated with the honor of outstanding senior in music education. This was the world of music. I had arrived. I was an adult and had to be satisfied and rewarded through fine performances, good programs, and just knowing that I had done the best I could. Still, I felt tension in my shoulders and inhibitions in my music, and there were no models of using music for transformation around me.

By the time I was twenty-three, I was polysaturated with musical knowledge. I felt inhibited about the many things I could not do well and wondered if I really wanted to do the things I did do well. I did not voice these feelings much. It was clear that I needed time to teach and just be musical. I began improvising and composing for some modern dancers who continuously suggested that I forget what I knew about music and simply watch their movements. If I would trust my deeper musicality, the sounds would emerge naturally from their movements.

I had the chance to go to Haiti to work in a children's hospital for ten days. It was the first time in my life outside of a music school. What a quickened world it was, full of sounds, movement, and intuitive music. The vocal sounds of the people were loud and richly textured, and they sang spontaneously with almost any melody or rhythm. The Haitians danced virtually all the time with graceful and rhythmic movements. Their congregational singing and genuine delight in music was transformational. But there was hardly a place for me musically in this musical country.

I returned for six months of volunteer work at the hospital. My French was sufficient, and I was glad to be out of music for a while. But soon an organist was needed at the Episcopal cathedral, so I began to help with the choir and play special services on a wonderful Austrian pipe organ. But the magic of the country did not open up until a friend took me to a full evening of drumming, dancing, and singing. I was caught completely off guard. For a powerful nine hours people danced with closed eyes and were healed. Everything pulsed, everyone danced just by hearing this primitive, complicated music. It was not exactly gospel music, but it was power, transformation, and the beginning of my awareness of the roots of elemental music. I went to these long night sessions only a couple of times in Haiti, but I never forgot the fear, delight, and fascination with the sound that went back in my memory farther than childhood. It felt rooted to my soul. There were now long, long, long sounds almost drowned out by powerful drum beats. They were somehow familiar, but I knew I had never heard these pulsing, throbbing tones before.

The months of tropical air, no study, and invigoration brought on the idea of going to Asia to my mind. In a few months I was in Tokyo rubbing shoulders with millions of people. A large French Canadian Catholic school needed a part-time elementary teacher. One year grew to seven. A few classes grew to a humanities program, a fine boys' choir, handbells, and a course on "The Great Books and Ideas of the Western World."

I began to observe the children on the playground, learning their rhythms and games. I watched the way they taught each other without a common language. Long talks with their teachers gave me important clues as to how these five- and six-year-olds were listening and learning. One teacher said if it were not for music she could not teach students because of their wide variety of native languages. She was not a musician, but she had mastered the art of tonality in her speaking voice and the essential power of rhythmic speech. Slowly it all began to come back to me—how I learned music. The rhyme, the rhythm, the gesture, the movement. The experiences that came before the whole note and notated songs were reemerging.

I spent seven years teaching all twelve grades. Actually, I spent more time in learning to restructure my own ability to listen than in preparing fine vocal ensembles. Thus, I began to understand the scope and sequence of music, but with the added value of many ethnic, religious, and musical backgrounds. I was learning something more important than I was able to teach, but I had no words or techniques to name it.

During those years in Japan in the 1970s, I was awake and open to multisensory ideas. The use of percussion instruments spoke to the children's bodies as much as to their ears and mind. When we used improvisation on specific modes, I could sense that we were evoking patterns of perception and emotional feeling that were far beyond anything I had read about in contemporary music journals on learning and music. This felt like an answer, but I did not know what I was trying to ask.

It came time to go home, back to my roots, with this array of realizations. A decade had passed since I had lived in Texas. I was offered a position as coordinator of workshops and director of education for a large organization devoted to sacred music for children. It was an opportunity both to continue working in the world of children and to deepen my studies in sacred music. The first few years were exciting and I was enthusiastic, but seldom were they inspiring or profound.

It soon became clear that I could not feel music in a totally Eastern or Western manner. Somewhere in the new paradigms were keys for music to regain its power to transform. I knew that there were ways to merge the varied musical experiences in my life without giving up the joy and delight that each one brought. I knew I had to make way for new dances and new ways of thinking that were not recipes, formulas, or popular psychological gimmicks. I had to take time to make music again, to feel music in my heart, to be swept away by the power of Mahler, Bach, drumming and Japanese folk music. I was dry, wounded and needing just to be with music and its power.

My doctor found a questionable lump in the upper left part of my lungs. He said I was under too much stress and needed to slow down and relax. A degenerative bone disease was also suspected. Finally, on New Year's Eve in 1981, I became enraged at myself, at music, and at the whole quiet pain within me. I wrote a powerful letter to myself saying that I was tired of being asleep. I stood on my desk and began to pound my hands and feet on the ceiling and desk, making yuletide thunder. Soon my eyes were closed and I was dancing in rhythm, a loud extended rhythm coming from my voice. A long, long, long tone began to whisper through the pounding feet and hands. And for hours it continued, becoming louder and clearer with every movement. I danced for nearly the whole night, belting out emotions, fears, tensions, grief, joy. A total, exhaustive cleansing! Something deeper than the *persona* came out. East and West wrestled. The system and the freedom tackled each other, without speech, thought or analysis. The spirit lifted me up, and I danced with the mild complaints of Job and the joy of a child. It was ritual, it was cleansing, it was healing. The power of music as a therapy, a wholing tool, took over.

I spent the next two days alone, sitting in quiet, listening to the St. Matthew Passion and Indian ragas. They were like ointments soothing burnt skin. My inner world felt tender, vulnerable and childlike. I wept, not from pain, but from freedom from pain. I could take deep breaths. My chest did not hurt; I just felt the fatigue in my legs and mind from the vigorous charge. I knew I was being born again as a musician. I had not yet found right notes or right reasons, but I had found the right feeling. I continued to rest. When I returned to the doctor; there was no sign of the lung or bone problem.

I began to listen to myself. Not to my inner chatter and judgment but to my inner music. I spent hours in sound and silence. I began to realize how these simple, powerful tools of breath and sound alter blood flow, skin temperature and stress. There were modes and rhythmic patterns that made the body feel relaxed after a few minutes of listening. Playing Bach slowly and noticing my breath patterns brought me immense well-being. I was getting in touch with those long, long, long tones that had touched me in Haiti, France, and Japan. I was transforming.

During this period a book called *The Metaphoric Mind* showed me that we had two conscious brains working together to give the remarkable result of consciousness. The system was on the left side of the brain and the tone and beauty on the right. I was recovering from a battle of these lobes. Soon I was taking some introductory courses in neuroanatomy.

I found that the left brain/right brain theories were already dated and being replaced by triune and holographic models. Suddenly, I was looking at a whole puzzle and a few fragments at the same time. This was music. It cannot be frozen and live. When a small part is analyzed, the power of the whole leaves. If the fragments are not strong, the whole piece can collapse. It was the correct metaphor for me.

I wrote a book of multisensorial exercises to spur interest in the brain. Puzzles, exercises, games, and playfulness dominated the approach. It was the first culmination of putting brain, body, and spirit into the dance. Simultaneously, I began to use a series of exercises to compose music. I began using my whole body as an ear to hear itself. I created pieces that were full of tone, subtle rhythms and harmonics that I could hear inside myself. Sometimes I used traditional harmonies, other times only harmonics. I began to feast on sound, tone, and breath and to realize and name the inner power "for keeps."

This book has come to me through exercises in my search for the "Ain Soph Aur," the sound of the limitless light. Any *book* about sound and music is a feeble attempt to relay power. But by using few words, space, and mindfulness to bring forth the true intention, the following pages may serve to release the power in each human instrument to enter into the core energy of thought, mind, and being.

We can learn to pull back from the outer senses in order to find a still mind and to explore aspects of our true inner nature. Yet, at times when we "go deep," we lose consciousness and miss the awareness of the passage between these states. Balinese shamans declare our human role is to link the living earth and the living heavens. I believe the power of breath, heartbeat, and vocal sound is the conscious link between body, spirit, and soul. Exploring the inner world through vibration is the most easily available and grounded way to learn of the spirit. It does not require study, travel or devotion to a guru. It is held clearly in each breath, each heartbeat and each utterance.

To enter into the initiation of sound, of vibration and mindfulness is to take a giant step toward consciously knowing the soul. There are hundreds of accurate models for this great journey inward. Each requires belief and discipline as well as the will to allow the inner and outer worlds to relate. Listening, learning, study and practice are important tools. But we need the courage to enter into ourselves with the great respect and mystery that combines the faith of a child, the abandon of a mystic, and the true wisdom of an old shaman.

Exploring the inner world through vibration is an easily available and grounded way to learn of the spirit. It does not require study, travel or devotion to a guru. It is held clearly in each breath, each heartbeat and each utterance. It is simple. We need only to have the courage to see God within ourselves as a unique reflection of all time, knowledge and ever-abundant love.

Boulder, Colorado
March 21, 1989

How to Use this Book

Each of the following chapters is divided into three sections. A depth of understanding of the text depends on the experiential meditations and exercises. For optimal awareness of the potential of sound and vibration, I suggest that you spend a week on each chapter. Begin each day by practicing the meditation; then read the text the same day. Then do the exercise. Continue with the same meditation and exercise each day that week. Reread the text when necessary, and repeat the exercise as you wish. On the last day of the week, review the impressions of the entire week and reread the whole chapter.

Each meditation is designed to prepare your inner world and thought for the ideas and information in the text that follows. We in the West have often lost the art of contemplation and meditation because of the rapid rate at which we assimilate facts and information. These meditations have been designed and tested to bring about an inner focus before introducing outer thoughts. To be able to sit with a thought, a concept, sound, or color for a prolonged period before you fill your consciousness with the ideas in the text will greatly enhance the depth of understanding of the information and exercises. I suggest that you spend half an hour holding the images or sounds in a waking, alert state before going on to the text and exercises. Without the exercises, you will not experience the depths of vibratory awareness that can make sound an empowering inner tool for self-discovery.

The diligent participant in this inner pilgrimage may wish to record some of the sounds made during the meditations and exercises, using an audio cassette. It is also of great value to keep a daily journal to record impressions, dreams, and contemplative thoughts that arise after the exercises.

1
Awakening Vibratory Awareness

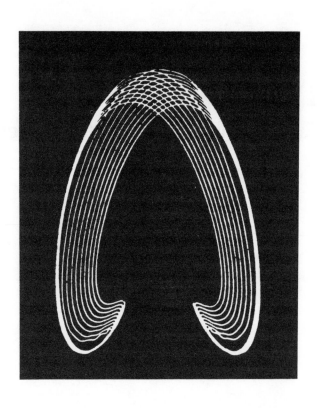

Meditation: Sacred Breath, Sacred Life

Sit comfortably in a chair so that your spine can relax upward. Close your eyes and visualize your whole body as a balloon. With every incoming breath, allow your whole body, the balloon, to expand slightly. With every exhalation, visualize your body releasing air from all its pores. Don't be concerned about having too much or too little air in the balloon.

Visualize each breath sending oxygen to every part of your body, from the tips of your toes to the top of your skull.

Experiment with the rate and depth of your breathing. But focus primarily on the round balloon image of your body expanding with each inhalation.

Meditation Sound: Each time you inhale, silently repeat the word "Breath."

With each exhalation, silently repeat "Life."

You may wish to concentrate on "Life" as you inhale and "Breath" as you exhale and note whether this is more comfortable for you.

Awakening Vibratory Awareness

Even within our most silent and still moments, there is a remarkable amount of motion within the physical body. The flow of the blood, the cycles and rhythms of the breath and heart, the billions of cellular motions in the tissues and organs throughout the body all create a symphony of motion beyond our auditory range. The autonomic functions of such processes as digestion, hair growth, transmission between the cells of the nervous systems flow with more rhythmic precision than our conscious minds could ever control at one time. If we were aware of all these systems, we would have little ability to focus on the outer world.

To explore our vibratory awareness, we need to approach our physical bodies with a heightened sense of listening. Our normal states of mind are hardly sufficient to penetrate the depths and heights of human perception. Great mystics, keen clairvoyants, and yogic masters have experienced a variety of channels through which the human mind can perceive dynamic dimensions outside normal consciousness.

In the most elemental and basic sense, each person is a musician, subconsciously conducting many systems and organs within the body. Even the most complicated counterpoint of Bach does not begin to approach the complexity of the cellular activity within the body. Only a few people possess the gifts necessary to become great composers or performers, but the essential musical qualities are *always* available within the body. The challenge is to let go of the traditional inhibitions that keep the rhythmic and tonal parts of us from transforming into sound and movement.

To listen deeply within is to awaken the musician. Inner music need not be refined or eloquent to be majestic and beautiful. No one would challenge the splendor of the Grand Canyon because it does not have perfect balance in all visual angles or because it does not match the proportions of a splendid man-made cathedral such as Notre Dame in Paris. The human voice, the breath, and the heartbeat are the elemental, natural environments through which the spirit and soul are expressed. It is not necessary to make our internal landscape self-conscious. Wounded musicians who were told they could not sing in tune or play an instrument well may have lost their glorious birthright of knowing the powers that are already in play. To become a great composer, a well-known opera singer, or a concert pianist is only for the few people who serve the refinement of the arts for humanity. To require a devoted worshipper to be a priest or Gothic architect is to disempower faith. The same is true with music. To require sophisticated education in performance, theory, and history can inhibit that awesome abandon to sound that is healing.

Language evolves out of a young child's inner motivation to reach out, communicate, and express emotions and needs to the outer world. If our only intent were to teach young children the sonnets of Shakespeare in the English of his century, most children would not be able to communicate with their family and peers. The inhibition of personal expression, creativity, and concrete learning patterns prevents the natural, joyous expression possible for children. Every child learns to speak primarily to communicate and thus reach out to the world. To judge a child's elemental expression in terms of Shakespeare would be to stem the evolutionary potential of new, and hopefully important, expressive forms.

This is so with music, but in a more rudimentary way. Every step we take, every utterance, every thought has a pattern, a rhythmic pattern which is energized by breath. The mystery schools of sound knew the vital importance of the connection between spirit and body. They used patterns of tone, movement, and breath to open the inner gates where awakened energy could flow between the subconscious and conscious worlds. The awakening of these inner and outer worlds does not come from overstimulation. It is not a frantic realization. It is a burst in seeing, listening, and feeling every part of life in harmony and balance.

There is a story about a young monk who asked the Buddha why he was the Buddha. "Is it because you have mastered all your desires?" "No," was the reply. "Are you the Buddha because you can levitate?" Again, no was the answer. "Because you can know all things?" Once again, the simple answer was "no." "Then, why are you called the Buddha, the Enlightened One?" The Buddha's response was, "I am only awake."

Only Awake! Fully able to respond without attachment. This seems impossible for the educated Western mind. But it is not a state of thought or non-thought. It is a state of vibration, resonance, and clear attunement and atonement with all that is. It is the condition of the awakened body-mind in harmony with all other energies, inward and outward. It is the highly awakened state that does not get caught in judgment, criticism, or egotistical self-consciousness.

One day after a music class for young children in Tokyo, a seven-year-old boy came to me with a joyous expression on his face. He asked me in a very sincere way, "Mr. Campbell, would you like to hear the first part of my very most favorite song?" I nodded positively and he proceeded to sing, "Doooooo." That was all, nothing else. Just one tone held for a brief second. He turned away and skipped down the hall, having expressed a great truth. I was startled because I realized that all favorite songs could be sung from that one note. I felt a Zen monk had given me the perfect koan or musical riddle.

Seldom do we give ourselves the privilege of such elemental simplicity without an apology. Western society has not embraced simple human observations and expressions because of fear of boredom in repeated experiences and patterns. We also think that if we did the simple things long ago, we must now be stimulated and evolve to become articulate and more "human." But the depth of the well is never boring. We can experience the grand "Ah Ha" in every pattern of our life. Just look for the first note of the song and sing it with full power, gentleness, and trust. Then the next note will come.

The challenge in developing vibratory awareness is to allow perception to be free, not bound by our enthusiasm to find out what will happen. The supreme joy in simplicity is to let go of self and see, feel, hear, and deeply sense what is happening. To observe and participate in the breath is to be in the midst of the happening. There is no stress regarding the outcome of the breath, the purpose of the breath or the thought, "Will there be a next breath?" The breath is on its way. The breath oscillates between two points, the height of inhalation and the depth of exhalation. It is the basic wave form of prana, life force, and human consciousness.

With the exercises and images that follow, it is possible to explore in safe ways the great elemental truths that support the spirit, soul, and body. Now begin. Just take a deep breath.

Exercise: Toning the Body

It takes great courage to focus on the subtle energies that surround the physical body. The perception of soft and nearly silent sounds demands acute concentration. Yet to begin to feel, see or hear these powerful and generally unacknowledged energies, we need to let go of some of our patterns of paying attention to the sounds and movements of the body.

Begin this exercise by speaking to your conscious left brain:

"My friend (the cognitive and linear part of me that is rational), I have a challenge for you. Can you be content to be out of the conductor's position so that I can explore the sounds of the instruments? Just allow the rest of my mind and body to explore what kinds of sound are available. Yes, I agree this is primitive and you might be embarrassed to be around such silly sounds, but there is great benefit in it. Just know that you can really help me by not inhibiting my exploration."

Once your left-brain self gives you permission to explore, begin:

1) Sit comfortably and close your eyes to enhance your listening skills.
2) Take a comfortable, unforced deep breath. Start humming a deep and very long sound. It does

not matter if the sound is high or low. It does not matter if it is beautiful or on pitch. The intention of the hum sound is to vibrate the body.

3) Now allow the sound to move slowly to a higher pitch and then back down so that the pitch rises and falls.

4) Place the palms of your hands on your cheeks and begin to feel the sound. Think of your hands as fully receiving the vibrations of the sound.

5) Spend five minutes making the sounds, then with eyes still closed, bring down your hands to your lap and just "sense" your body. Take a few minutes to be awake and aware of how the body feels in the quiet. Then make the hum sound for another five minutes.

6) The left brain will remind you that time is up, that you have had plenty of time to fool around, and that this kind of exercise will not accomplish much. Comfort that conscious conductor by stating that many cognitive challenges and interesting perspectives are coming in the following chapters and that later you will give time for linear, logical thought.

2
The Wounded Listener:
Balancing Inner and Outer Sounds

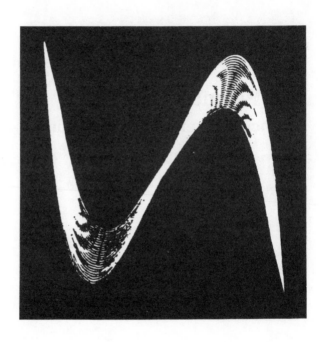

Meditation: The Pulse of Life

Sit in a comfortable position in an extremely quiet place. Even a fan, a neon light, or a clock can be distracting in this exercise.

Observe the breath as you did during the previous meditation. After your body and mind feel still and you are fully aware of the breathing pattern, begin sensing the pulse of your heart throughout the body. Be aware of the many patterns and rhythms of your heartbeat.

Visualize each beat as a golden spark of life force. Sense it as if it were a silent, gentle lightning pulse throughout your whole body.

Meditation Sound: Silently repeat "Hah." Keep your mind centered on the inner sound "Hah" while sensing how the beats of the pulse affect it.

The Wounded Listener:
Balancing Inner and Outer Sounds

Words cannot always be trusted. Words mean too many things to different people. If I listen with my feelings, then I understand what others really know about life. If I listen without my feelings, then I understand what others know about things. My teachers grade me on things. I do not think they remember how to listen to feelings. All this confusion about learning and grades! My grandmother taught me that feelings were more important than facts or things because with them I'm connected to my life spirit and my ancestors and all the animal healers.

Most of my teachers and friends do not remember that words alone are not enough. So I do not trust the way others hear my thoughts. I can listen to their words and their hearts, but they do not understand my language. I think I'll be quiet until I can be heard without words. It's easier to communicate by drumming and singing.

An eighth-grader from Liberia

I remember my great-uncle Tom. He was always old when I knew him, but he looked like a little boy. He had no teeth, wore overalls every day, and spent his retirement years humming while working around the house and garden. He was in his seventies when I was a child. In my eyes Tom was different from everyone else in the whole world. He did not speak, although he was neither deaf nor mute. He simply got mad one day when he was twenty-two and told my great-aunt that he would never speak again. And that was it. He adopted a language of silence.

I often think of him and wonder if he forgot how to think in our everyday language. He always seemed happy, kind, and fulfilled. Now in prolonged periods of concentration and meditation, I wonder if ceasing my speech for three decades would make my inner conversation with myself louder, quieter, or slower.

Children are often confronted with the frustration of not being understood. Because they do not have enough control of language, it is difficult for them to know how to say things, how to communicate ideas and information, and thus be really understood. Emotion is carried in the tone of a child's voice. Finding the right words to match one's feelings is an awesome challenge. As children grow into puberty, discovering sensitive words or expressive art forms becomes important as a bridge for their inner world to reach out to the outer. As adults, we don't always know exactly how language and feelings fit into this inner world. We often trust our pets as patient and understanding listeners more than we trust our parents and teachers. The tones, language and gestures we use with pets are richer with emotional expression than our average conversations with each other.

As children, we were in closer touch with our needs, our emotions and our desires. The body was not dissociated from thought. Normally we were intensely aware of the physical sensations of pain, pleasure, color, sound and smell. By age eight, we were told to sit still to learn, be quiet when thinking, and develop intelligence with a pencil, a book and our eyes. The natural rhythms and patterns of the body were put on hold for six or eight of the best hours of each day. Many of the feelings, sensings and powerful knowings that were becoming familiar were forgotten because they were not named, mentioned, or developed into mature expressions of thought.

We learn to be unsure and afraid of our natural powers, yet the lost child in each of us yearns to speak or reach out into the world—if only we could be sure of being heard and understood. Uncle Tom may have been childish and stubborn in his decision to become mute for the rest of his life. But the betrayal of not being heard, of not feeling in harmony with others, was so real that he made a drastic decision to survive by silence in the family and in society.

Counselors, ministers, and therapists hear clients utter these phrases repeatedly:

"He never listens to a word I say."

"My parents never listened to me."

"If only they would listen."

"My employer will never listen to us."

"If I have told my teenager once, I told him a thousand times."

"Nobody understands me."

This two-sided sword implies that when we are not

heard we are not clearly communicating. We feel separated and long to "get things straight." The distance between the feeling and the words we use can become so great that we find precious few words to say what we feel. It is difficult to communicate even with ourselves when words limit our ability to sense our intuitive and symbolic thoughts. Words become weak, inadequate reflections of feelings. Our cognitive response does not have a deep enough feeling. It can move so fast that any sense of the "pure mind" of Buddhism seems beyond the reach of our own daily mental activity. We feel disharmony with our inner state. We postpone getting to know our deeper self through listening: "If only I felt better physically." "If only we had a new administration." "If only I had more money." "If only I were married." "If only. . ."

There is an energy underneath these thoughts. It does not use words. It motivates us to find words, or it automatically envelopes thinking with words without sensing the origin of itself. Our language is losing meaningful words and replacing them with technical terms that are necessary but not expressive.

If we were to listen for the emotion within the words themselves, could we not better listen to each other? Our subconscious registers all the inflections, but we seldom value their meaning. We miss seeing all that's there. We miss listening to what's there. While watching the Olympic diving competition, I was amazed by what I missed within each dive. The acuity of the judges' eyes perceived details in the dive that I could hardly observe even in slow motion. The same alertness to tone of voice is of value when listening. True, it is possible to become so focused on the tone that the general meaning is lost. But it is significant to learn from the inner power of the voice as well as from the surface meaning of words.

Every cell in the body lives in a rhythmic pattern. Every organ has its cycle and pulse. Life energy itself moves through the body upon the breath and heart-beat. This life-rhythm never stops, yet it alters and balances itself every minute of the day. The conscious mind cannot hear all patterns, but they are powerful, never ceasing, louder than most outer stimulation received by the sensory parts of the brain.

For example, within the inner ear are tens of thousands of small hairs or cilia in the spiraled cochlea. When they become damaged by extended exposure to noise and loudness, they cease to function, and the brain begins continually to create the sounds the damaged ear can no longer hear. This condition, called tinnitus, is also common when the nerve cells in the cilia begin to age. Loud never-ceasing sounds or ringing within the brain result from the disabled ear.

The inner world of image, color, and kinesthetic feeling is also more apparent when there is no outer stimulation. The sensory parts of the brain that operate during dreaming are different from the parts used in conscious awareness, but the sensations they give rise to are real. These inner tones, gestures, and colors have become familiar to the mystic, to the contemplative listener, and to creative people. The awareness is deeper and more powerful than thought; it is an acute sensing in an awakened, powerful internal space.

Until early in this century, some people experienced

these inner senses through a variety of altered states of consciousness. They were called the fever, the Vitus, ecstasy, the vision, trance, or the Dreamsong. The powers of the psyche that were tapped deeply could result in initiation, healing, ecstasy, terror, or in revelation. Within these altered realities, demonic, angelic and spiritual powers flourished. The messages from these states molded the psychological and social as well as the religious behaviors of cultures that honored them. If religious practices were mystical, the society could more easily move from the inner realities into the outer world. There were fewer intellectual and technical manipulations of the earth and society because reality was a balance between the rhythms of inner belief and social action. Ritual and music created venues between these inner and outer worlds. Even within charismatic Christian communities today, there is a healthy remnant of these altered states through the unity of movement, glossolalia and singing.

With the rise of more cognitive, technical societies that de-emphasize mystical religious practices, the bridges between the conscious and subconscious have been slowly weakened. With the introduction of chemicals, electromagnetic fields and mechanical rhythms all around us, the sensing mechanisms that flow between one world and another have become callous. When television replaces children's imaginative play times and safe independent places for developing are invaded with high-tech sensory stimulation, children begin to lose their natural, intuitive connections.

The wounding of our listening abilities is more than the feeling of not being heard. It is a wounding of the integrity of a deeper, more powerful self that must

35

have a healthy life to maintain balance in the physical and emotional parts of our nature. It is easy to become tangled in an endless maze of cognitive patterns. Phrases lose their power by constant and unemotional use. It is just as easy to become caught in an emotional pattern that cannot be aptly expressed in words. The final danger is falling into an intellectual pattern that is cognitively so well insulated that there is no room for new thoughts outside of that pattern to evolve. Important inspirational insights can come to be regarded as strange little psychic cartoons that pass without significance. When the lid on our inner rhythms and powers becomes too tight, immense pressure builds. When the lid is blown off too abruptly, as through drugs, a dangerous wounding may occur that damages the ego's ability to stay intact.

The great fears that develop through being cut off from society and family are based on the greater terror of being separated from the powerful depths of our own intuitive, subconscious perceptions. When we refuse to listen to these deep, unknown parts of the psyche, physical and emotional tensions emerge that that lead to an imbalance of perception and thought in the outer world.

The depths are again beginning to rise. Public interest in bringing the inner senses back to consciousness is apparent in the attention given to stress-related diseases, psychological services to the public, and new forms of spiritual involvement based on intuition. The popularity of channeling and meditation shows the need for these inner states to appear. Fundamentalism, both political and religious, also rises with the same intensity as the depths of the psyche. Whether the fundamentalism is Christian, Muslim, or Hindu, it seeks to repress the evolving depths of perception.

In nature, when any species of plant or animal refuses to adapt to new conditions, it begins to atrophy, and within a few generations it dies out. On the other hand, if the organism changes too radically and abruptly, it cannot adapt to its new form and begins to weaken. Similarly, we need to find a healthy way to adapt to our changing world. We have the choice of becoming stuck in patterns and fighting for their survival or beginning to look at the vast realities within and to find them reflected in the outer world.

Health is balance, balance between the inner and outer worlds. Listening is active awareness of both worlds. My uncle Tom may have made an extreme choice by muting his words. But he was heard more clearly than others in the family who consciously knew little of the inner need to be deeply heard.

These chapters and exercises create an opportunity to bring rhythms of the inner world into balance with the outer forms of awareness. To read these short chapters without the inner exploration is to miss the power of this book. Respect that inner listener, even if it does not feel wounded. That unlanguaged self deserves your undivided attention, if only for five minutes a day.

Exercise: Healing the Listener

Sit comfortably, with eyes closed, in a quiet place where your body can be supported gently. Spend three minutes breathing deeply, with the intention of making more room to listen within your body. Allow each inhalation to bring in more inner space and better acoustics for inner listening. Allow each exhalation to release tension and cluttered or disorganized thought.

After three minutes, begin to tonalize the breath with the vocal sound "Ah." Continue to make the "Ah" sound on the exhalation for a couple of minutes. Then allow thoughts about the past twenty-four hours to emerge. As you review the past day, start with this exercise and progress backwards through your activities and associations. Begin to observe the emotions that arise when you ask yourself, " Was I heard? Was I understood?" The answer is not a yes or no but a non-judgmental sensing. Remember to keep breathing naturally but deeply with the tonalized "Ah."

Now allow yourself to go deeply into situations when you felt wounded. Think of a time when you felt unheard, unnamed and frustrated. Go gently into this vulnerable or awkward time and allow the "Ah" to fill the place in your body where the wounding occurred. Allow the tonalization of the sound to release the emotion. Use the power of the breath and your own sound to heal that wounding, the pain of alienation. Even though you may not have consciously felt the pain at the time, release it now with your voice.

Then bring your mind back to a calm place. Use the "Ah" to fill your body and mind with a clear and vital sound. You may wish to image the opening of a window on a clear, beautiful day with the "Ah" as fresh air clearing the room.

Please reread this page at least three times before you begin the exercise. The last section is by far the most important because it clarifies the experience. When you have finished, stretch and spend a few minutes walking outside, moving to some music, or exercising lightly. Give your body time to integrate the rhythms and patterns.

3

The Energy Beneath Sound:

Sound Waves and the Brain

Meditation: The All in Every Sound

The very first sounds of human life hold a charged power. They declare the pain of life and the sound of breath.

There are also sweet sounds that intimately bond a parent and child. The lullaby, rhythmic rocking, bouncing, and play all pattern physical and emotional relationships.

In this meditation imagine yourself as the parent of a small, contented baby. Close your eyes and begin to hum to the little one, at the bottom of your voice. Allow it to slightly rock your body. Don't sing. Just vibrate your breath with a closed mouth and deeply relaxed hum. Feel yourself enveloped in soothing vibration.

Key Words for Meditation: I am held in the safety of breath and vibration.

The Energy Beneath Sound:
Sound Waves and the Brain

For many years it has been popular to try to achieve "higher" or "deeper" states of consciousness. Many believe that knowledge of great mysteries and truth comes through these altered states of awareness. If we do achieve an awakened experience, we may spend years trying to tell others about it, or analyze it for comparative religion's sake, or try to name it in scientific terms. Once we think we have it, then begins the dilemma of what to do with it.

This way of handling experience is part of our Western pattern of social and cognitive exchange. How can we at the same time be both part of social patterns and rhythms of thought like this and apart from them? The left brain hardly has a clue as to how this might occur. But we all have an intuitive nature that can know without naming.

Dr. Paul MacLean, M.D., a neurological researcher at the National Institute of Health in Washington, D.C., has created a model for observing brain functions that is of enormous value for learning about parts of our intelligence that are not cognitive. He has divided the brain into three sections: a) the old autonomic hindbrain; b) the emotive, bonding midbrain; and c) the newer left/right frontal areas of the cortex. Students of esoteric thought can easily see the correspondences between this view of evolutionary brain development and the writings of H. P. Blavatsky, C. W. Leadbeater, Rudolph Steiner, and Max Heindel.

The brain can be compared to a unique symphony orchestra. The lowest part of the brain, just above the brain stem, is classified by MacLean as the "reptilian brain" because it has many similarities to the brains of alligators and snakes. This area of the brain is automatic in response to the needs for food, shelter, mating, and territorial rights. Unthinkingly, "fight or flight" typifies the natural responses of the reptilian

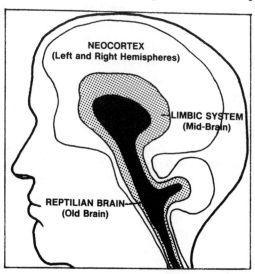

THE TRIUNE VIEW OF THE BRAIN

The black area represents the brainstem and oldest part of the brain found in reptiles, mammals and humans. The midbrain area in grey represents the limbic area found in older and evolved mammals. The white area represents in left, right and pre-frontal lobes, the newest part of the brain, found in mammals.

brain with non-emotional attachment. The strong urges to protect our homes, maintain our bodies, hunt and grow food, and procreate come from deep below our conscious thoughts. As we consider the natural abilities of animals, fish and birds to find food and to build protected homes and nests, we can sense the patterns of our intuitive, automatic life-maintenance systems. The rhythms of the mating season, of hibernation and of eating reflect the deep-seated unconscious urges of this part of the brain.

The basic power of music is in the rhythms of the physical body. Walking, running, breathing and the ever-present roar of our pulse create the elemental beats that underlie the sonic world. Folk dances and songs reflect different beat patterns and linguistic tonalities in each cultural region. These unique combinations are developed by the natural environment, climate, food, and the amount of physical activity of each unique social and regional group. By listening to the rhythmic patterns that underlie the folk expressions, we can begin to know the "body" of that culture. Today, especially in the United States, we can observe the amalgamation of many traditions. Even in the popular music of a country, we can observe many qualities coming together and coexisting in an art form.

The mid portion of the brain, sometimes referred to as the limbic system, regulates the tone or emotion of the body. Although we know that language is not formulated in this old mammalian part of the brain, it is here that the most basic sounds of expression are made. Cries of pain and joy and deeply emotional inflections issue from here. The humming sounds of a mother to a young child, the sucking, hissing, and sighs made to our pets, and the loaded sounds we make in emotional states of deep grief or ecstasy reflect this sonic intuition that lies beneath cognitive language. These expressions are understood intuitively.

In this midbrain area is a part of us that yearns for bonding, family, and social belonging. Reptilian behavior, originating in the older hindbrain, would lead to mating and then leaving the newly born young to the fate of nature. Mammalian behavior, originating in the midbrain, leads to nursing and caring for the young. Our natural urges to belong, whether to a family or a nation, stem from the old mammalian brain, the midbrain.

When we chant or hum for long periods, we can stimulate this limbic area to reduce stress and give us a sense of well-being. Toning creates a deep sense of being bonded within ourselves. We can reach a state of contentment in a safe and fully aware state of mind.

We use this area of the brain to consciously communicate with our basic natural rhythms. It is the gatekeeper between the conscious and subconscious worlds. It is the seat of the emotions, the fears, the joys, the longings that may not be in our conscious knowings. If we experience an emotional trauma, this area can become so vulnerable that the ego closes down emotional responses in order to stay in control. There is no conscious sense of time here, but there are temperament, mood and the tone of our conscious responses.

The anatomy of the brain may not seem relevant to the musical or artistic aspects of life. Yet by understanding how different the intelligence and function of these neural areas are in regulating our listening and communication responses, we can begin to orchestrate different levels of our thought into greater harmony. The inflections in our spoken language, the power underneath our words, and our potent longings to reach out from the inner "motions" to the higher states of awareness in the neocortex are all controlled by mind— this universal and archetypic regulator of inner and outer worlds.

Music affects the midbrain through the conscious awareness of the higher areas of the brains (left, right and prefrontal lobes). Music also influences our behavior and health through the rhythm and tone pulsations that directly affect the lower parts of the brain without the higher brain centers realizing it. The limbic system is the gatekeeper between two inner worlds, the sleeping and awakened parts of each of us that must live together in our human personality.

As we move up into the conscious parts of the brain, we find the well-known left and right hemispheres. It is true that we have two brains in the conscious mind, but we should not be misled into thinking that they are the only significant parts of our mind/body/spirit. Without a doubt, they are the easiest to understand, because they are the parts of our waking selves that we know and can usually control. Dr. Jean Houston's song about the right and left brains is an effective and rhythmic chant that easily explains some of their awarenesses and functions:

Left Brain, Right Brain

Left brain, right brain • get your head together.
Left brain, right brain • get your head together.
Get • • • your head • • • together.

The left brain discusses what your eyes can see,
Teaches you to read and the one, two, three.
The left brain helps you structure your day,
If you didn't have a left brain, you couldn't say
That the right paints pictures,
Right brain loves stories,
Right brain makes scriptures,
And right brain dreams glories.

Left brain, right brain • get your head together.
Left brain, right brain • get your head together.
Get • • • your head • • • together.

The right brain intuits things as a whole,
Synthesizes, integrates, believes in the soul.
The right brain visualizes patterns so strange,
If you didn't have a right brain, you'd never change.
And the left brain clock watches,
Left brain loves order,
Left brain hates blotches, and the
Left brain makes borders.

Left brain, right brain • get your head together.
Left brain, right brain • get your head together.
Get • • • your head • • • together.

And the corpus callosum acts like a road
For the two brains to share each other's load.
In one given second there's a quadrillion things
That the brain puts together and that's how it sings.
Whole brain wants teaching.
Whole brain needs learning.

49

Whole brain's out-reaching.
The whole brain is yearning.

> Left brain, right brain • we'll get our heads together.
> Left brain, right brain • we'll get our heads together.
> We'll get • • • our heads • • • together.

After you have read this song, read it again aloud while tapping your foot or clapping your hands. The sign * indicates a slight rest. Notice how differently the meaning comes to you when you read words rhythmically.

The simple dichotomy of left brain, right brain is partially true. We do think in a dual fashion. But we have a million ways to use conscious perception. We can no longer hold onto a simplistic view of two brains. All parts of the brain and body have different functions and manners of performance, just as do all the members of a great symphony orchestra.

These brief and simple descriptions of the brain are not meant to explain our consciousness or spiritual nature, just as the instruments in an orchestra should not be confused with the music. The spirit of the music transcends components of the written score, the composer, and the performer. The spirit within us transcends all the parts of the brain. But understanding the variety of instruments within the brain can be of great use.

The prefrontal lobes are in the newest part of the brain. This area is the front area of the neocortex, in the forehead. It is made up of parts of the left and right hemispheres, but it has a unique quality. It can see full patterns, processes and procedures. It is able to sense the beginnings, middles and culminations of activities. It can understand words such as humility, justice, love, empathy and compassion, words the left brain can define but not completely understand in a concrete way. This is a conscious, prayerful part of the brain. It is the third eye, third ear and spiritual mind of perception. It can respect all life, sense holistic patterns and coordinate vastly complex activities. It is the conscious conductor of the neural symphony.[*]

The parts of the brain are closely related, connected, and intertwined. Unlike a symphony orchestra that is directed by its conductor, the brain is coordinated by all of its sections simultaneously through conscious and unconscious synaptic patterns. Music, rhythm, pulse, and breathtone can integrate the parts of the brain efficiently, non-invasively, and quickly. Tonal vibration can instantaneously modify breath, blood flow, emotion, and cognition. Inner music can synchronize thinking, feeling, and physical states.

As we learn consciously to respect and connect the patterns, needs, and responses of the different neural areas, we can begin to evolve into more harmonized people. Again, music can physically and emotionally bring diverse systems of body/mind patterns into a harmonic balance.

As above, so below.

----

[*]For a fuller description of the development of the creative brain, see Don Campbell, *Introduction to the Musical Brain*, St. Louis: Magnamusic Baton, 1983.

Exercise: Exploring the Depths of Memory

One of the high mysteries is memory. How do we recall patterns and events? What is our remarkable ability to dream, to sense and name experiences? As we have explored aspects of the brain, let's also explore patterns and information that are held within our bodies. This kind of memory is usually not available to the conscious mind unless accessed through physical movement, deep sleep or altered states of awareness.

Most physical games, musical instrument playing, and patterns of speech are built upon repetition, so that a natural response can be performed spontaneously without laborious thought. Repetitive movements or sounds leave the conscious left brain quite bored, and it shuts down. It questions the need for repetition without a practical application, such as walking, chewing, or digesting have.

In this exercise you will move from an elongated tonal pattern into experiencing the thought process that creates memory patterns. As in many forms of meditating or playing an instrument, the early stages are sometimes difficult. There is a tendency to feel that real proficiency will never come, that distracting thoughts prevent you from carrying through until new patterns are firmly established. Be patient and know

52

that the difficulty in the beginning is natural, essential part of building new patterns.

Close your eyes and begin to make the sound "Nahn, Nahn, Nahn, Nahn." Stay with the repetition for fifteen or twenty minutes. Notice the vibration within your body, the places where it is vibrating. Begin to be aware of your breath. Try not to think. Just allow the sound to carry itself. After this prolonged period, begin to think of the different parts of the brain.

As the sound continues, think of the many meanings of "Nahn." What could it mean in different languages? How could it be spelled in English? How many other words can you associate with it?

Then spend a few minutes sensing your physical feelings and your emotion when you made the sound without thought. Did the sound evoke a particular emotion?

Last, begin to sense the position of your tongue in your mouth. How does it move to create the sound? What muscles are used? What is automatic and what is done deliberately? Which automatic parts of the brain must function to create this sound?

Now go back to making the pure sound without thought, but this time with the intention of staying awake and being more aware and alert.

Now come to silence. Just sit quietly for a long time and sense the bottom of the breath, where it starts and where it stops. Record any special realizations or insights.

4
Toning, Chanting and Singing

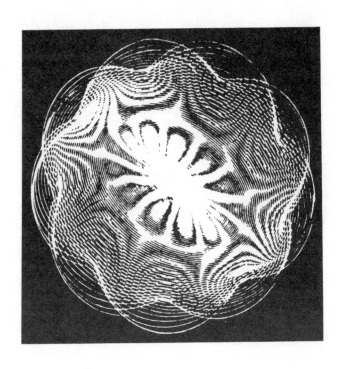

Meditation: Aaah-Haah

The "ah-ha" experience is that moment of insight that flashes into the mind after we have given up puzzling over it. "Ah-ha" also occurs in meditation and contemplation. It is the moment of awareness when we put together thoughts or questions so quickly that a sudden, dynamic realization takes place.

Without making any audible sounds, begin by taking deep, relaxed breaths. Sit in a comfortable posture, allowing your body to be upright but without stress. Close your eyes and concentrate on making long inhalations and exhalations without any force.

If your mind strays and becomes cluttered with thought, just gently focus on your breath. It is quite natural for a variety of thoughts to enter the mind. Allow them to pass through without becoming attached.

When your breath is natural, slow and in a steady rhythm, begin visualizing each inhalation as "Aaah" and each exhalation as "Haah." Imagine the moment of awakening as an "ah-ha" experience occurs as being stretched out and prolonged in time.

Stay in this focused meditative state for fifteen minutes a day throughout the week you are working with this chapter.

Toning, Chanting and Singing

The early Greeks and East Indians were in touch with the power and mystical qualities of tone. We cannot adequately express their understanding of the Word, the Logos, the thought that originated creation. It is loaded vibration. It is empowered movement. It is the first expressive awareness. It is the moment when creation first knew itself.

We are constantly naming and labeling things according to our physical sensations and making logical deductions based on them. In the rapid process of clothing thoughts in words, it is a challenge to observe what brings the thoughts themselves into being. Similarly, in moving from a quiet breath to a tonalized sonic vibration, the exact beginning of the sound is difficult to catch. Once a sound is made, however, the power and awareness of that sound takes over. It is not possible to put the millisecond of beginning on hold. If this micromoment is shortened to the instant the sound is executed, the sound escapes and there seems to be no real tonal content.

In the beginning was the Word. What was the beginning of the Word? Was it a short instant outside our earthly sense of time? Or was it the very instant of the beginning of time? In Greek, *logos* means not only "word" but also "sound." Word, sound, light and thought are critically linked to the beginning of all knowings and namings. Each is a sibling to the others, in neurological, philosophical, and theological contexts. Yet if we imagine an actual universal or cosmic acoustic occurrence, we lose the energized power of the sound.

Sound waves vibrate in the atmosphere around the earth, and our ears respond to a certain range of these frequencies. There are hundreds of thousands of inaudible frequencies above and below our hearing range. Our ability to hear higher pitches diminishes with age, so that children hear a wider sonic range than their grandparents.

If we could hear all audible sounds simultaneously, it would sound like a constant stream of rushing roars. The crashing sound of a waterfall, the breaking of massive waves and the rush of violent winds produce a vibratory chaos, stimulating a full spectrum of energy carried through the ears to the brain. This would be similar to the sound of the flow of blood in our veins and arteries if we could hear it all at once. If all sensory information were sounded together without any neural discrimination, the brain would roar. If we were aware of the stimulation in the millions of complex nerve sensors, our conscious minds would open to such a large stream of chaotic information that we would have no way to sort out meaning.

Sometimes our sensory mechanisms are not working normally, and we cannot name and access information through inner speech. Thus, we generally assume that we do not perceive it. But not consciously hearing sound does not mean that we do not receive the sonic stimulation in another manner, through our skin, hair, and bones. The vibration is there, modifying the air around us. There are also other forms of perception, not generally available to our sense organs, that are available to clairvoyants, clairaudients, and psychics. Our lack of perception does not mean that these forms of intuition and communication do not exist and are not readily associated with nonconscious parts of our brains.

When one of the conscious senses is defective, others become enhanced so that communication between the inner and outer worlds can be more facile. Without sight or hearing, Helen Keller was able to develop patterns of communication through speech. Her inner world was rich with thought and pattern, even though she was not able to receive sensory information from the outer world in normal ways. Each of us can enhance our sensory abilities by readjusting normal perceptual patterns and exploring ways to extend awareness.

Sound is basic to many cosmologies of the earth's creation. For the Hindus, all was dark and quiet in the womb of the universe until the first movement, which created the sound "OM." This cosmic vibration is so strong and so subtle that all things in the universe are dependent on it. From this sound, music was created. From music came dance, language and drama, where stories of joy and tragedy were translated from the realm of gods to the human world. In Indonesia, the king of all gods created a giant gong. When struck, it became the bridge between the Creator and the created.

In Japan when the sun goddess went into full retreat into a cave, there was darkness and no life on earth.

When the first sounds were made, she came out of the cave and new life began to manifest. In every cosmological myth sound and music are a major link between God and the people of the earth. In Bali it is sound that creates the link between the worlds. The magical sounds of the elemental spirits, the secret languages of the animals and totems, the secrets of the shamans were all held in the sounds of the drums, rattles, and sonic invocations that arose from the depths during dreams and visions. Our modern mind has become so cluttered that it keeps us away from the sources of power and enlightenment on which every text of wisdom insists. Are the healing powers of David's harp no longer strong enough to heal cancer, stress, and heart conditions? Dare we try the tonic that has been so freely given to us and so obviously forgotten?

The energy underneath sound, the power that increases before a thought emerges and our ability to intuit information are the keys to an exploration into tone and vibration. How can we reach this unnamed potential without an endless agony of doubt or easy infatuation with the novelty of a new system?

The left brain alone is not capable of knowing the answer to such a question unless one experiences tone-making for prolonged, uninterrupted periods. Yet during the tone-making, the left brain can easily become bored, uncomfortable, and critical. To read about these ideas may be of interest from a left-brain perspective, but there is little power in words about sound without the inner vibratory experience of sound itself.

The guidelines provided in these meditations and exercises bring discoveries that cannot be found through logical thought alone. Exploring silence and the very beginnings of sonic vibration within the body requires stillness and discipline. To understand the power of tone demands a series of personal experiences through which thought becomes united with the physical tonalization of breath. Thinking about and understanding the concepts is a weak tool compared to the healing power of uniting thought with breath.

In modern styles of music, elongated tones are seldom found. Experimental composers like John Cage, Gyorgy Ligeti, Peter Michel Hamel, and Brian Eno are often more interested in the tonal composite of sounds than are in the lyric, melodic forms of music more familiar to the listening public. Often the public feels that these sonic sketches fall into categories outside of music. Even folk music does not utilize the power of tone to communicate its emotional content.

Tone is simply any audible sound, prolonged long enough to be identified. In old French *ton* and in Latin *tonus* mean "sound." In Greek *tonos* means "stretched." We use these meanings interchangeably to signify any sound or any elongated sound. "Toning" is defined in this book as the conscious elongation of a sound by using the breath and voice. The word "tone" is also commonly used to mean the brightness or darkness of a specific sound or color; the condition of a specific organ in the body; or the pitch of different words in a tonetic language such as Mandarin or Bantu.

To "tone" the body generally means to stimulate or invigorate health. A "tonic" can be prescribed to balance the body. This is also the primary purpose of a vibratory sound made within the body for the benefit of the body itself. Novalis, a German poet-philosopher, said, "Every disease is a musical problem. Every cure, a musical solution."

Could this imply that any function of the body can be stimulated and normalized through tone? We have ample opportunities to observe that traditional and classical styles of music do not evoke the same response in all people. Taste and style change radically through the centuries. The dissonance of one century became the harmony of the next. Novalis recognized that we can use sonic vibrations in a harmonic context to heal the dissonances within the body. Our own toning sounds, not necessarily interesting, beautiful, or creatively organized for an audience, can vibrate, massage and balance the body without any invasive methods.

This kind of sound-making is different from the sonic methods now used to entrain the brain waves through headphones. It is vastly different from the specific sounds a shaman makes to assist in the healing process. Originally, the early forms of sacred chanting were forms of toning that expanded the power of the words of prayer and scripture to center the mind, breath, heartbeat and energy systems. To quickly evolve toning into chanting or singing is to take away its natural, vibratory and healing character. These more evolved forms of sonic release and artistic expression are essential to culture, but they cannot replace the power of the sustained tones themselves.

Gregorian chant from the sixth century, with its phrases that elongate a single vowel sound on several neighboring pitches, demonstrates the evolution of tone as it began to merge with text. The rough and elegant combinations of tones and their high sonic colors, as found in Tibetan and Mongolian chanting, reflect the potency of sound and its virile, male nature while containing sacred, magical texts. Although every vocal and instrumental sound is made up of overtones (colors), those in Tibetan and Mongolian choirs are easiest to hear. In America and France, the Harmonic Choir, directed by David Hykes creates an artful and eloquent sound through overtone singing. The enchanting sounds in Ligeti's *Requiem*, used for the film *2001, A Space Odyssey*, achieve the haunting use of vocal tones as a sculpture in time without dominating rhythmic patterns.

To an educated musical ear, this attention to tone itself may seem too primitive to create meaningful aesthetic content. But without experiencing toning for an extended time, one cannot know the importance and validity of this book. There is no way to convey it in words; it is experienced. The bibliography lists a number of brilliant books about sound, music, vibration, and their philosophical and esoteric natures. Such information is amplified and validated by the exercises, not by adding more viewpoints about sonic powers.

When a tone is sung or played on the same pitch for extended periods and then other sounds, melodies, or pitches are made above that basic sound, it is called a drone. Drones produce psychological grounding. The drone becomes the "earth" of the music, the place where one walks and lives and where all the foods necessary for sustenance are grown. Even in musical terms, it is referred to as the "ground" of the music. Music not based on a continuous drone also has a "tonic" or root, from which the other sounds move in and out of harmony. Students of musical harmony and physics will recognize that the fundamental of every note is a type of ground to its overtones.

Scottish bagpipes, Aboriginal didjeridus, and Indian tamburas all create a tonal ground upon which music develops. Yet there are hardly any instruments that can produce so pure a tone that higher tones are not simultaneously produced. It is the unique combination of the overtones and colors that allows our ear to discern which instrument is being played. In American Indian music and much African music, this psychological ground is induced rhythmically by drumming.

Each room in modern homes and businesses is permeated by the drones of the lights, electrical appliances and computers. They have a strong influence on our moods and sense of well-being. The brain becomes entrained to sounds after a short period of time and literally does not hear them. Yet the body is always aware of the sound. We are made aware of the dangers of inaudible low-frequency drones from power lines above our homes by the alarming upsurge of cancer in those who live nearby. These rhythms are so out of harmony with the earth's drone of 7.8 vibrations per second that people between this sound and the earth incur disease. Begin to notice the sounds of the refrigerator, television, computer and automobile traffic each day. Such sounds are always there, even if not consciously heard.

By sounding one's own body, it is possible to give it a tune-up. Singing is a good way to start, but most songs do not sustain a sound for a long enough time to reap its benefits. To tone for ten to fifteen minutes a day can greatly change the way the mind and body work together. When the body is healthy, all the systems and organs are in harmony and without pain. The body's natural function is to grow and to balance and continually to heal itself. By allowing sound to move into the body through the breath, the life force can activate, vibrate and restore balance within.

Musicality is not important in this toning process. Actually, it may be more difficult for trained musicians to let go of the artistic aspects of music. At first, music activates the right side of the brain above the ear. After music literacy, tonal discrimination and performance interpretation develop, the frontal area of the left lobe begins to dominate the listening experience.

For five years I served as music critic for a newspaper. I was concerned with the quality of performance, interpretation and historical accuracy. I remember many times when I was irritated at a performance that fell short of my standards. Yet the person next to me was having a transformative experience through emotional rapport with the music. I was the loser. My knowledge stood in the way of deeper, more powerful aspects of the music. I began to realize that I was hearing more music, listening more critically and enjoying it less. Could there be a way to allow the power of the sound to move me deeply without sacrificing the ability to discriminate?

Only when I began studying the different manners in which the brain listens could I reconcile these diverse ways of listening. The endorphine release of quieting hormones that many times accompanies goose-pimpled moments of joy is more available when the analytical left brain does not consciously dominate the right and midsections of the brain. When we develop a more open and natural state of listening, the left and right hemispheres become more integrated and balanced; this will allow the central portion and hindbrain to receive the musical benefits.

Modern uses of toning were intuitively developed by a minister in Colorado, Laurel Elizabeth Keyes, after she began to sense the remarkable powers of the voice in healing. She experimented with her congregation and friends in the 1960s and wrote a book to introduce her experiences. In *Toning, The Creative Power of the Voice*, (DeVorss, Santa Monica, 1973) she recalls her initiatory moments with sound:

> This practice of Toning began for me one day after a study group had gone and I was standing alone in the room, enjoying the stillness and the charged atmosphere of such a meeting. I noticed a sensation in my chest and throat as though a force were rising, wanting to be released in sound. It was the feeling that might cause one to burst into song, for no known reason, or to gasp as one might when coming upon a beautiful scene. I observed this as it rose and subsided, almost a thing apart because certainly I was doing nothing to cause this. It had a volition of its own and an apparent desire to express. It was an odd experience to both watch it and feel it, without making any effort to direct it or control it.
>
> I found my lips parting and my mouth opened very slightly in an easy relaxed manner so that the teeth were just barely parted. Unexpectedly a sound bubbled up, like something tossed up on a fountain spray. A Sung syllable emerged—*"RA"*.

I couldn't have been more astonished. I did not use Egyptian terms and we had not been discussing that culture. Why the sound took that form was as bewildering to me as if some other foreign language might have sprung from my throat. It came up again, paused as though frightened, but when it was not stopped it came out and soared.

I would liken it to a bird that had been caged all its life and found the door of its cage opened. It tried its wings, scarcely knowing what to expect, and finding it could be lifted in flight, it flew in delighted abandonment.

The feeling was as though these sounds came from the earth itself, and poured up through a silver tube, through my throat, effortlessly, freely as artesian water flows from the ground. I did not take a deep breath, as a singer, but the note was sustained as though supplied by a limitless source and it went into heights that I couldn't have reached normally since my voice is rather low.

I know of dozens of such experiences of vocal release. The emergence of such free expressions are natural when the conscious brain does not inhibit these moments as useless or unsafe. Actually, the flow of subconscious releases is quite natural and very regular in the life of children, of highly creative people, and of mystics during a state of rapture. It is also a regular activity for many with neurological and psychological disorders. We naturally suppress such expressions for fear that we, too, might become imbalanced.

Some of the primary functions of the voice are so instinctive and intuitive that we hardly know how to fit them in an acceptable social setting. As soon as we begin our early childhood education, we are told to sit still, be quiet, listen, and think. We learn to inhibit some of our audible sounds before we are able to hear them clearly inwardly. It is beneficial to tonalize and improvise sounds as we learn. Doing so provides important memory patterns, and these can incorporate our emotions into ways to hear ourselves think. This may be a vital clue to the mystery of language development in some new forms of education where movement, tonalization and drawing are seen as essential to developing memory.

The exercise at the end of this chapter begins to bring our sonic nature into vocal manifestation. When we try to judge the beauty of the outer sounds we make, we inhibit their awakening. "Toning" is here defined as the vocal sounding of the breath, no matter what the pitch or quality.

There are not many examples of music that stay on one pitch for long without a special text or syllable to enhance the tone. Usually rhythmic patterns are played around the long tones, or another voice sings a variety of notes in a chant or melody above it. Tone alone has not been of great interest in the history of music. But many religious traditions use repetition of tone to help focus the mind. A simple text may be repeated many times to stabilize the breathing patterns and the mental focus. Generally called chants in Western culture and mantras or mantrams in the East, these repeated sequences quickly bring together vibration, thought and breath.

Until the Protestant Reformation, prayers were both a personal intention and a cyclic memorized series of phrases, spoken, chanted or sung. The long periods of repetition allowed the body, mind and emotions of

devotees to rhythmically synchronize. The more enthusiasm or spirit integrated with the prayer, the more
engaging it became. By observing the rocking motion
of the Hassidic Jew intoning prayers at the Western
Wall of the temple in Jerusalem, the Tibetan monk
chanting the sacred texts on multiple tones, or the nun
reciting the rosary at Lourdes, it is easy to see how the
use of repetitive sound awakens the inner world of
spirit. A bridge between the inner and outer worlds begins to be built, and the power of faith is amplified.
There are hundreds of different practices of chants
throughout the world, and although seemingly
unassociated by their outer sounds, they are all methods for engaging the inner powers naturally receptive
to spiritual activity.

I am not advocating potent forms of trance for all
Western people. That would be inappropriate,
invasive, and perhaps harmful. Yet we have developed
such strong, logical, left-brained constructs to control
the outer world that we may have lost our natural
awareness of how to harmonize and work with the
inner world. The use of our own sounds to knock on
the doors of perception is safe. It is dangerous to inhibit the flow between the subconscious and conscious
minds. To be in a Black gospel church during the glorious singing of a rhythmic hymn that repeats itself with
increasing vigor for ten or fifteen minutes, or to be in
Roman Catholic communities that use the melodic
chants of the Taize tradition is to enter the ever-
flowing cycle of sound. African drumming, Central
American shamanic singing, Balinese dancing, and
North American sacred harp singing are but a few of
the rich religious traditions that invite the inner and
outer worlds to blend and harmonize simultaneously .

If we use phrases or texts repeatedly, the sounds and rhythms of the words evolve beyond their definition. I had a strange experience during high school when in drama class I was given an assignment to say the word "pull" two thousand times. I realized that I was putting more thought into counting than into the word itself. So I counted how many times I could say the word in thirty seconds. I figured it was about eighty times per minute; I could repeat the word for half an hour and do the exercise fully.

That evening when I began the strange challenge in my room, I entered into a world of sound beyond meaning, and meaning beyond sound. Later I discovered it was similar to some of the experiences common to Zen monks. I felt the word, I explored it throughout my body. It was such a curious exercise that I never got bored. I became aware of the rhythm of my tongue and lips. I imagined the shape of the air in my lungs, larynx and throat. I thought of a dozen ways to spell the sound, say the sound and change its meaning by the inflection in my voice. I wondered why there were two *l*s in it. I divided it into syllables. I modified the vowel sound. I stretched it. I noticed how different just thinking the word was from speaking or chanting it.

I had been "pulled" into a new reality with words and sounds. I never lost the meaning of the word, but I came to realize how elusive the word itself is. All words hold the same power to disappear into sound and then reappear with meaning.

In India the mantra holds the power to connect words and their meanings to potent spiritual and psychological insights. *Man* comes from *manas*, meaning intelligence or consciousness. *Manas* signifies our ability to distinguish ourselves as knowing, thinking and feeling beings with the capacity of reflection. *Tram* means a protectorate, the shade or wings that surround us with safety. It also means a crossing path, a way to move through consciousness. Thus a mantra is a way of being held in knowing, safe with understanding, in close harmony with oneself. Mantras are composed mostly of short, simple syllables, such as Om or Hum, arranged in patterns so that their meaning relates to a sacred text. There are many ways a word holds meaning. When we go beyond the meaning of a word and feel its sonic pattern, we approach its power.

Chanting probably first developed from repetitive movements, such as walking, chopping, utensil crafting and farming. People probably improvised sounds to create a breath pattern that matched the movement. If a movement is repeated many times, a melody, a word chant, or some tonal activity begins to emerge. The pulsation of that pattern usually falls into groups of two or three beats. Syllables begin to form. The railroad songs, the seasonal planting songs, as well as the early childhood songs in every society, have this power of repetitive pattern. These vocal patterns make the job go faster and more easily. When sung in groups they create a rhythmic bonding among the people making the sounds.

The oldest vocal repetition and chanting are devotional. Uttering the name of God for long periods or repeating part of a prayer or sacred text were used to help develop concentration and deepen spiritual bonding, healing or intention. To intone the holy names and become receptive to their powers is the foremost function of these early mantras. Mahatma Gandhi spoke of the mantra as one's very staff of life: "It carries one through every ordeal. It is repeated not for the sake of repetition, but for the sake of purification, as an aid to all effort. It has no empty repetition. For each repetition has a new meaning, carrying one nearer and nearer to God."

The repetitive "rap" or chant is used in early childhood education to help children memorize. Chanting the alphabet, the multiplication tables or the spelling of words reflects back to primitive ways of chanting words or letters in a pattern. This repetition of syllables becomes implanted in the subconscious parts of our minds and influences our memory and thoughts.

The heart and power of a mantra is its seed sound essence held within the vowel. In Sanskrit, the *bija* (or seed) is the basis from which meaning, intelligence and devotion grow. The mantra's power is based on planting these seeds into the whole rhythmic breath pattern. Each seed sound has a power that can be used for healing. Wise teachers knew how to combine these seed sounds into rhythms that balance, clear and transform the body and mind.

The seed mantras hold little meaning. Their purpose is to emit the power of the sound. These phonemic improvisations of seed sounds are easily heard in the American Indian chants such as "Hey-ya-ya, Ho-ya-ya, Hey-ya-ya." When the seed sounds are emphasized within sacred texts, the meaning and power of the text are amplified. These powerful patterns set into motion the vibrations necessary to modify internal blocks in the psychological and physiological systems within the body. They also "open the ears of God." Lama Anagarika Govinda, a German who became a Tibetan monk, speaks of mantras as primordial sounds that are archetypal word symbols. "All mantras are modifications of an original underlying vibration which sustains the whole energy pattern of the world."

While toning is usually extended breath and sound on one tone, chanting can include a variety of tones. Usually, however, mantras are one, two, or three tones with one acting as the anchor or root of the others. It is common to start and end on the same tone, moving to one above and one below for the inflections. It is easy to hear the tonalization and chanting elements in a reading voice; the repetitive patterns in the voice are a form of chanting. This close association between thoughts, actions, movements and speech demands an acute ability to observe the senses without being distracted by them.

There are over a hundred recorded systems that correlate the use of tones, colors and rhythms to spiritual keys that balance and unlock powers within the body. Few of these agree in specific detail, but they are all based on this awesome power of tone that can connect us to ourselves, to each other and to the spiritual powers that await our desire to know them.

Vilayat Inayat Khan, foremost Sufi teacher, wrote about the power of sound in a number of brilliant and inspirational books. In his book *The Music of Life*, his words are as clear and powerful as any written on this subject:

> Work with sound until you are absolutely amazed

that you can produce such a sound and it seems to you that you are just the instrument through which the divine pied piper blows the whisper of the incantations of his magic spell. . . .Become yourself a pure vibration beyond space. If the sound generated by the vocal chords into the vibratory network of the universe has the faculty of tuning one, it is because it links one with the cosmic symphony. The repetition of a physical sound sets off a sound current, a vibrational tidal wave in the ether, by building up energy. . . .You must become pure vibration and pass on through to the other side.

Commentary on sound and music as part of spiritual development is common throughout the world. Yet it does not feel concrete enough, in this complex technical world, to fulfill our left brain's need to be thorough and linear. The only way we can know these things is to try them, not learn about them. We may not all have opportunities to travel, visit sacred sites, study with master teachers, or even receive the education necessary to qualify us for better positions. But we all have the power to go within and discover the power of our own breath. It takes no teacher except courage.

Sing the song of the soul. Let it rise from tone. Let it rhythmically flow into its own life. Let it become You. To sing another's song is to rob the other's power and your own. Move your own body to its rhythm. There is danger in singing someone else's song. The unnatural spirits will enter your body then. Just sing yourself over and over. . .you'll be purified.

I have paraphrased this advice from African musicians whose musical power I witnessed. These words may hold more truth than we can reasonably imagine in a contemporary musical setting. To sing is not enough.

We must tap the powers that lie beneath the consciousness of the song. The song leads down to the chant, the chant leads down to the tone, the tone leads down to the breath, and the breath leads to the energy beneath the sound—the roar of silence.

Exercise: Awakening the Sonic Spectrum

Sit comfortably. Begin to relax and breathe deeply.
As you close your eyes, exhale and make the sound
"Whoo" without opening your mouth except for a small
area in the middle of the lips. After you have found the
place where this vibrates the chest and throat gently,
then begin to move the pitch upwards. Let it glide up
and then glide down. There is no scale, just a tone slid-
ing gently up and then gently falling. Experiment with
the sound for five or ten minutes. See how far up and
how far down you can make it without any strain.

Now repeat the same procedure with the sound
"Why" for five minutes, and then with *"Whee"* for another five minutes. Notice where the vibration is most
powerful in your body, where it feels best. Notice
which thoughts and emotions appear.

You can discover the sonic spectrum of vibration
within your body by feeling the response of your
sounds with the palms of your hands. You will easily
detect the power of your breath to vibrate different
parts of your skull and body.

This exercise is of enormous value. To spend a
month exploring how different sounds in high and low
registers directly modify the vibratory response in the
body has great benefits for health and curative educa-

tion. Toning awakens a powerful memory in the body
that is beyond our conscious left-brained awareness.

5
Transformation through Sound:
Effects on Body, Mind and Spirit

Meditation: The Sound of Peace

Sit comfortably with your eyes closed and begin to observe the flow of your breath. After a minute, begin to think the word "Peace" with each inhalation and exhalation. As you inhale, feel the meaning and power of the word flow in through your breath to the lungs and through the blood to all parts of your body. As you exhale, think the word "Peace" as being released into the physical world.

After five minutes begin to sound the word "Peace" as one long tone with each exhalation. As you inhale, silently think and feel the vibration of the word. Allow your mind and body to focus and charge themselves through the thought and sound. You may wish to explore the lower, middle, and upper parts of your voice as you tone the word.

Transformation through Sound:
Effects on Body, Mind, and Spirit

All life is vibration. Each sense responds to distinct vibratory energies around the physical body. If you imagine the senses as drumheads of different sizes made of a variety of materials, you can see how different vibrations enter into your physical field of perception. The eye is receptive to specific frequency ranges, the ear to others. Responses to different frequencies are directed through the skin, bones, eyes and ears to the brain. The receptive abilities of your eyes, ears and nose allow the outer world to enter your inner cosmos. Touch and taste are far more immediate and physical. They respond to the closer, more intimate vibrations around us.

Sight, sound and smell are our connectors to the extended world. It is common to see tens of miles into the sky and across the earth on clear days. We see our own bodies whenever our eyes are open. The bridge of the nose or the brows peripherally frame our every glimpse of the outer world. They consistently obstruct our full view.

While sight gives us a directional focus of what is in front of us, hearing is a multidirectional tracking device that completely surrounds us. The subtle acoustic environment of a room gives us a vivid impression of how much space is there. Gothic cathedrals made of stone are "alive." In them sound travels, reflects and bounces off thousands of surfaces, creating an enormous vibratory environment. When we make sounds and tones or sing songs in such an ambient space, we feel our sonic power. The sound can hold us, or better, we can hold ourselves in our own vibration. The same is true of those magical tones in the shower that reflect our great operatic power, no matter how limited the range.

If we close our eyes, the vibratory motion of the air creates an image of the space we are in. The sonic reflection is determined by the temperature, the humidity, the room size and the depth of our breath. Our earlids are not as easily shut as our eyelids. Even though we may not consciously listen to all the sounds around us or pay attention to the information held within the words spoken to us, our sonic, vibratory receptors are attuned to the space around us and affect our sense of well-being. The unnoticed sounds literally tell us where we are and how we can balance ourselves between the inner and outer worlds.

Our ability to hear is many times more agile than sight in perceiving and discriminating fine details. When light is flashed on and off in rapid sequence as in a motion picture, we cannot perceive the interruptions. If the rhythm of a visual pattern is very fast and has equal spaces of darkness between the projections, we do not even notice the emptiness. While we slur visual information that is less than 1/50th of a second, the ear can discriminate intervals between sounds at 1/500th of a second. Morse code operators are five times quicker in recording messages through sound than through light signals.

The ear is so vastly complex that volumes have been written on its physiological, neurological, and esoteric natures. To understand the potency of tone and vibration upon the body, it is necessary to develop a mental image of this remarkable sensor.

Alchemy is a metaphor for the journey of sonic vibrations from the cochlea of the inner ear to the different parts of the cortex where sound is processed for musical, linguistic or aesthetic evaluations. All the elements found in alchemy are used as conduits through which sound passes. From the outer element of Air, sound enters through a funnel into the cave where the

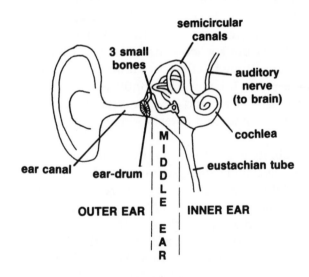

THE EAR

The three parts of the ear translate vibration through air, bone and skin into auditory information for the brain.

eardrum resonates three little bones made of the element Earth. These three bones in the middle ear are the only ones in the body that are fully mature in size at birth.

This midear system oscillates rhythms, patterns, and pulses into the deep regions of the inner ear. The delicate spiraled nautilus of the cochlea, filled with fluid and tens of thousands of tiny hair-like cilia, transforms the vibratory elements of Air and Earth into liquid, the element of Water. This fluid does not circulate through the cochlea of the inner ear but stays within its tiny space. Yet this part of the hearing organ looks like a swirling liquid vortex that is naturally produced in a rushing stream.

Hans Jenny, Swiss scientist and artist, took remarkable photographs of the influence of sonic vibration on a variety of fluids and particles. His pictures show that sonic impulses directed toward liquid at rest immediately produce spiral vortices which look very much like this part of the ear. It seems that the ear itself developed out of sound for the purpose of knowing sound. Here in this inner chamber the powers of frequency dance and transmit energy from the outer world to the brain.

The sound patterns make a long chemical and electrical journey from the inner ear, through cranial nerves, to the brain centers where the sonic vibration is connected to conscious knowing of sound as a sense. Here the element Fire comes alive as the electrical charges of nerve impulses leap across the gaps between nerve cells. The ear performs the alchemy of gathering, transforming, and reforming vibrations and then formulating them into sound. The inner fluid, with its resonant powers, reflects the harmonies of the universe, the music of the spheres. The ear and brain filter out many sounds so the information can be translated into thought. This filtered sonic information chemically reconstructs outer vibratory stimulation into inner audial information.

It may be that the primary function of the ear is not hearing, listening or the sonic entrainment that gives us the sophisticated ability to discriminate subtle differences in sounds. The ear gives us the power to know space and to sense our relationship to motion in every direction. The three semicircular canals in the inner ear serve as a gyroscopic guide to our position in space. The liquid within these canals moves with every slight movement of the head, telling us whether we are upright, prone, or in between. Some lower animals have only one or two canals, and this limits their directional discrimination. In humans these canals intersect and turn back upon themselves in such a way that an upright posture is possible. It is sensible to think that this part of the ear stimulated the brain to evolve. Without the sophistication of the inner ear which permits an upright posture, the growth of the newest part of the brain, the prefrontal lobes, would not likely have occurred.

Even though we may not discriminate higher pitches, we have the ability to hear, analyze and recreate harmonics, counterpoint and the tonal blend necessary to language development. The ear was developed and shaped around sounds. The patterns, pulses and powerful energy of life created a need for the inner perceptions of consciousness to conform to already existing outer shapes. We think temporally and sequentially, and we have great difficulty in sensing and naming whole, patterned systems. Our mind cannot grasp all of a complex sonic pattern simultaneously. That would be like hearing an entire symphony in one brief second. Sonic patterns must flow through time so that auditory discrimination can take place. If all sounds were to coexist in our brains, we would hear endless, full-spectrum noise.

The sounds we hear today are vastly different from those of past millennia. The sounds that produce pleasure, beauty and release within the body are different from those that people responded to a hundred years ago. Musical instruments have evolved from primitive tubes, strings and pounded membranes to finely tuned keyboards and strings with exquisitely built wooden chambers to amplify the richest sounds. In the past twenty years, hundreds of thousands of new sounds have been developed with the electronic synthesizer and a new era of sonic stimulation has been introduced. The most fit of instruments have survived. But with the availability of recorded music from many cultures, we are beginning to evolve an appreciation of new patterns of music, sound, and speech.

Hearing modifies our sense of time. The psychological relationship between sonic stimulation and the passing of time is essential for tonal understanding. As vision helps us deal with space, hearing gives us the rhythm of passage through time. The presence of background noises gives us a sense of time moving. If we are in a fairly soundproof room, time does not seem to pass, even though light may give us a sense of day and night. The convergence of space and time is one of the high mysteries. The ear is the vital tool for the magic of balance, hearing and learning.

As music and speech began to develop from sound, we became aware of the finest perceptions in micro-patterns of time. No other sense can observe such fine details in a short period. But when the sounds are not musical or linguistic in nature, we cannot discriminate the patterns. When three or four meaningless sounds are made randomly, we can hardly tell which came first. Yet in the coded context of language or music, we have ways of remembering, knowing and naming that sequential information. The repetition of patterns, of phrases, and of rhythmic tones allows us to develop conscious memory. Thought itself is musical, that is, rhythmic and tonal, even though it moves so quickly that we cannot hear its voice. Cognition is formed by the rhythm of outer stimulation upon the inner field of the mind. The roar of thought without sound holds the power of knowing.

However, this is only one side of knowing. In Western societies, we have focused our attention on the effects of stimulation upon development and growth. Could we begin to sense the inner powers that imprint the outer world in our consciousness? The power to sense tone and sonic vibration extends from the inner sensing world to the outer world. We do not yet have instruments to measure this inner power of sensing, but there are clues to discover these energies. The inner sensing will emerge if we take the time, make the space, and slow down our outer stimulations. The mystic's inner sense of hearing, seeing, sensing and moving is as real as the senses that show us the outer world. As above, so below—as without, so within.

Time flows in and out of consciousness every day. We lose a conscious sense of local time when sleeping, but our body clocks know when morning and evening come. Many rhythms affect our sense of time. The rhythms of the heart are the most obvious. The brain waves, the cycles of the stomach, kidneys, and intestines, and physical movement create various rhythmic pulses, thus altering our consciousness.

After childhood, our perception of time changes. Children live in a perpetual now, in a concrete world. Each day we live, there is a slight shift in our sense of how long a day is, how time is connected to us and how we think in the sequential patterns of time. Time seems shorter because of its slightly diminishing proportion to all the previous days in our lives. We learn from patterns. We anticipate future time by recalling past times. Though obvious, these observations are essential to our exploration of sound, tone, and music.

The complex influences of sound on the mind and body are loaded with linear-time information. Yet there is a secret to sound that takes us back to the most mystical and existential state of awareness—the endless moment, *NOW*. This pattern is so short, its rhythm so concise, that we cannot hold onto it. We can hardly slice it down to its smallest size. Yet NOW is totally elastic. It could be based on one heartbeat, which might occur as slowly as every eighteen seconds or as quickly as three times every second. NOW could be timed as one breath, one brain wave, one moment, one movement. Or NOW can be a suspended feeling for an hour or an afternoon. Or NOW can be reduced to an endless millisecond. NOW depends on our rhythmic sense of time.

Without the rotation of the earth around the sun, without the moon and its cycles of reflections, without the seasons, without a clock, how can we define NOW? We write of universal time, cosmic time, eternal pulse and rhythm, but what are they? Are we able to tap into their pulses and patterns from our earthly rhythms? Are there any non-timed spaces and places? (Truly, we do go out of conscious time when we sleep.) These questions of consciousness are deeply rooted in the experience of sound and tone within our bodies.

I remember the first moment I discovered time. When I was five years old, my grandmother told me to go to sleep immediately on a summer night when I had been up long past my bedtime. There was a full moon, and as I lay down on my back, I could see the shadow of a tree on the wall at the end of the bed. I was wide awake, not at all sleepy. I blinked and the room was full of light. I was startled. I had not gone to sleep or awakened. I was robbed of knowing I was asleep. It was as if two tapes or films had been spliced with no fading or transition. I had never known time before that night because it had been continuous in my mind-body. But that night my illusion was interrupted. NOW had briefly stopped flowing into NOW. Time jumped and skipped a beat.

As we feel time pass or become caught up in the idea that just thinking passes the time, we hardly know how to extend the NOW into a fully present, awakened state of consciousness. Various forms of meditation and yoga teach methods for focusing on the NOW and thus allow pure mind and extended time to become a regular experience. Running and exercise, creative projects, and even mundane daily habits such as cooking and cleaning allow us to flow into rhythms that fit comfortably into our personality.

Through tone we can begin to elongate the experience of NOW, so vital for the balancing of our physical, mental and emotional rhythms. To sound the voice is to massage, oxygenate, and vibrate ourselves internally, from the inside out. Singing and speaking move the vibratory epicenters so quickly that there is no time for the body to balance itself with the sound.

The vowel sound that carries the vibration to the body determines the effect of the sonic charge. The pitch of the vowel sound determines the location of the epicenter. There is no other way to localize oxygenation, energy flow, and pulsation as noninvasively within such a short period of time. Yoga and meditational imagery techniques can create similar experiences, but only with years of discipline and training. While they may be more effective on the etheric and subtle bodies, even they do not move physical energy as readily. Stress, depression, fatigue and overexcitement can be transformed into an awakened and relaxed state with the use of sound. Within two to three minutes, the mind and body can be brought into a clearer, more balanced state.

The breath naturally releases expressions of joy, sorrow, pain, and confusion. But as children, we were taught to keep our sounds to ourselves. To hold in those sounds and store up those emotions is to push them into deeper subconscious states where they create tension and disease over extended periods of time. There are many ways to release the emotions, but the efficiency of sound to balance and deter negative emotions is extraordinary.

Through long breaths and with long tones, the body can be massaged from the inside out. Although the sounds may not be beautiful, musical, or even expressive, their use will immediately begin to balance physical and mental energy systems. When first experimenting with these sonic experiences, there is a strange sense of feeling awkward and slightly ridiculous. If you have done the exercises for a week from the time you started this book, toning will begin to feel more natural. But if you jump into experimenting without the gradual preparation of toning, you may well become as skeptical as the little boy in "The Emperor's New Clothes."

The power of sound upon the etheric and spiritual bodies, as well as the physical, is awesome. It became apparent to me many years ago when I was studying Gregorian chant. Although the sounds did not stay on one pitch for more than a few seconds at a time, the smooth, melodious phrases seemed to induce a sense of well-being and spiritual awareness. When I became familiar with some of the chants and memorized them, I could go inward and at the same time feel an extended awareness.

Many years later, the work of a French physician and ear specialist came to my attention. Dr. Alfred A. Tomatis's observations of the connections between the ear, the voice, and physical well-being have become paramount in sonic research. During a recent interview with Canadian Tim Wilson, he spoke of his use of Gregorian chant:

A few years ago I visited a monastery in southern France, which had been taken over by a new abbot, a young man. He had changed the internal rule of the abbey by modifying everything a little after the Second Vatican Council, and he was therefore something of a revolutionary. When I arrived, there were those who wanted to retain the Latin, others who were for the existing rule, and still others who wanted to change and revolutionize everything. Finally everything was changed. They even eliminated chanting from their daily schedule. You know the Benedictines chant from six to eight hours a day, but this abbot succeeded in demonstrating that chant served no useful purpose, and that without it they could recapture that time for other things.

Well, in fact, these people had been chanting in order to "charge" themselves, but they hadn't realized what they were doing. And gradually, as the days passed, they started to get bogged down; they became more and more tired. Finally they got so tired that they held a meeting and frankly asked themselves what it was that was causing their fatigue. They looked at their schedule and saw that their night vigil and the rhythm of their work deviated excessively from the norm for other men. . .and they seldom slept. They decided that they should go to bed early and wake up, like everybody else. . . [but after that] they were more tired than ever. So much so that they called in medical specialists to help them try to understand what was happening. They finally gave up on this after a procession of doctors had come through over a period of several months, and the monks were more tired than ever. Then they turned to specialists of the digestive system. One of the great French doctors arrived at the conclusion that they were in this state because they were undernourished. In fact, they were practically vegetarian—they ate a little fish from time to time—and he told them they were dying of starvation. I think my colleague's error was in forgetting that they had eaten as vegetarians ever since the twelfth century, which one would think might have engendered some sort of adaptation in them. Anyway, once they started eating meat and potatoes like the rest of the world, things only got worse.

I was called by the abbot in February of 1967, and I found that seventy of the ninety-seven monks were slumping in their cells like wet dish rags. Over the next several months I examined them, installed some machines to electronically reawaken their ears, and reintroduced their chanting immediately. By November, almost all of them had gone back to their normal activities, that is their prayer, their few hours of sleep, and the legendary Benedictine work schedule.

Chanting is a reawakening of the field of consciousness. At the risk of oversimplifying, hypnotic effects are those of relatively lower frequency which play on the more primitive areas of the brain. With Gregorian chant you are directly affecting the cortex, which controls the monkey rather than being led by him.

In order to avoid the awkwardness of having some monks with trained ears and some without, it was best to put them all on the same wavelength immediately. This is the situation you find naturally when they have been singing together for many years. There is an identical rising auditory curve, one which has undoubtedly been conditioned by the sustained breathing they do, and which makes for a unity that is hard to find elsewhere in the world. If you take two monks and charge their ears with opposite curves, they will immediately enter into conflict at the level of language. Thus, Gregorian chant needs perfect blending. If you give this sort of auditory curve to someone who is not a monk, he or she will become extremely aware.

It is impossible to arrive at this state of permanent consciousness, though, without having the opportunity of always being charged. And of course the environment of the monastery is a very important factor. The Benedictines are lucky in that they are vowed to silence. This is a verbal silence which keeps one from uttering conscious nonsense. But it is important, if you succeed in extricating yourself from this condition, that a strong stimulus be provided—for at least four and a half hours each day as I said—in order that one can meditate or work. That is what chant is doing.

In the past some monks believed Gregorian was to be sung like lyric songs. They pushed very hard and sang Gregorian as if they were singing Othello. But this is false because Gregorian is meant to train one to rise up out of the body. To give a sense of interiority, yes, but an interiority in the cosmos itself.

The chants of Tibetan Buddhist monks, Sufi dancers, and Christian Gospel singers have powerful charging effects on those chanting sound with one another. Yet if we do it alone, in our own private inner world, there is no danger of a group magnetism that may alter our true sense of self. When we are in tune with ourselves and develop sound health in mind and body, we can more easily harmonize with others around us and benefit from group soundings.

Each individual's body is tuned to several keynotes that change according to age, time of day, health and food consumption. No single note will attune the body indefinitely. The mind-body field needs to be tuned daily. It can automatically adjust to the emotional and physical needs of that moment. The NOW is constantly changing and eternally present.

The exercises and suggestions made here are introductory and general and also safe and healthful. No dogma or particular spiritual point of view is needed to make them effective. Yet they can amplify daily meditational and contemplative routines. Simply spend three minutes sounding before beginning your daily spiritual discipline. Then use the tools you already have without imposing another system for enlightenment.

At first, sonic experiences may seem strange and feel quite silly to you. You may have skipped over some of the suggested exercises in the previous chapters. But trying them is the only way you can find for yourself the profound benefit that sonic awareness can bring.

It is not possible for us to tone or chant for four hours a day as monks. But the remarkable benefits of charging the body, brain, and spirit are observable in a couple of ten-minute sessions each day. If it is embarrassing or impossible to make sounds while you are reading this book, you may have to modify the exercises so that you can sound in your car or while walking or in the shower. But I invite you to experiment seriously with the exercise at the end of this chapter, even if none of the others has seemed appropriate for you. You will benefit from this exercise, even without previous experience. It will give you ample opportunity to explore the vibratory powers of sound upon your body. By toning and chanting, you can consciously and safely approach the inner roar of life, the ever-flowing energy that supports every action, thought and feeling.

Exercise: Exploring the Vibratory Centers

Sit comfortably in a chair with your eyes open, placing the palms of your hands firmly on your head. One hand should be at the top of your head over the crown and the other firmly placed around the back of your skull. You should feel the pressure of your palms securely on your skull.

Begin to tone the vowel sound "A" (as in "say"). Begin fairly loudly at the lowest pitch in your voice and slowly rise to the highest pitch that is comfortable. Then let your voice fall slowly back to the beginning pitch. Rest a moment, and continue to the next vowel, "E," repeating the same sonic scan. Then continue with "I," "O," and "U." After making all the vowel sounds, close your eyes and sense your body. Notice its feelings, tensions, and energies.

Now with eyes closed repeat the same vowel sounds in sonic scan. This time be aware of the epicenters (centerpoints) of vibration within your skull. Notice how the pitches modify the vibratory centers and which vowels have calming or stimulating effects. Repeating these exercises two or three times a day for a week is most helpful in finding the sounds that are most charging, calming, and harmonizing for you. They may change daily. It is helpful to record some of the experiences for your personal reference.

6
The Overtones of Health

Meditation: The Wings of Song—
The Lightness of Sound

Stand with your eyes closed. Imagine that your hands are long enough to reach nearly to the floor. Then sense your arms and hands as great wings. Without moving your arms, imagine your wings flapping as you slowly raise them over your head into five positions:

1. Close to your side   Hmm

2. Extended at a 45-degree angle   Oh

3. Extended 90 degrees, parallel with the earth   Ah

4. Over your head at 45 degrees   Eh

5. Directly above your head, nearly touching your ears   Ee

Let these imaginary positions flow smoothly, slowly, and gently. Since your physical arms are not moving, there is no stress whatsoever on your physical body.

Now imagine your voice moving through a full vowel spectrum. Start with a "Hmm" sound, open slightly to a long "Oh," then "Ah," then "Eh," and lastly an "Ee" sound. These are easy to remember as they flow into one another naturally.

Although this seems more like an exercise than a meditation so far, it is vital to be comfortable with the movement images and the vowel sounds practiced separately. The next step is to combine them. You will feel how naturally and gracefully the movements fit with the sounds.

Now start the meditation. Stand and center yourself by taking four or five deep, slow breaths. Take another deep, relaxed breath and begin moving through the sonic sequence from "Hmm" to "Ee." As you silently intone each vowel, imagine your wings moving through one of the five positions: with "Hmm" arms down; with "Oh" arms raised to 45 degrees; etc. Mentally, keep the wings flowing smoothly and evenly. When you have finished the sequence, slowly move backwards through all the vowel sounds till you return to "Hmm," reversing the movements of your wings through the five positions. Take a breath after each full cycle and start again. Continue this cycle slowly for three minutes.

Sense the light, bright energy coming from your body. As you will discover, this is one of the most effective and significant meditations for health, balance, and well-being.

The Overtones of Health

A few years ago, eleven monks from the Gyuto Tibetan Buddhist monastery came to America to chant. On the day of their arrival, they performed their tantric ritual at the Museum of Natural History in New York. Their long horns, cymbals, trumpets, drums, and bells provided the liturgical orchestration for their sacred service. Religious vestments and holy paintings of Buddhist figures ornamented the stage for this historic event.

What began as normal chanting of a sacred text, in a rhythmic, full-toned sequence, suddenly dropped and expanded. A suprahuman sound—rough, elemental, and rich—sounded well below the ordinary range of the male voice. After the audience became transfixed with the unusual tones and seemingly unrefined sounds, there arose a subtle, bright expansion of a sound two and one-half octaves higher, in a range common to the finest boy sopranos.

The monks were not singing parts in harmony as we know it. Each was splitting his tones to produce two or three separate notes, including the earthy bass notes and the eloquent, flute-like sounds of heaven. Two worlds were resonating together. These sounds are said to "burn like fire" or "flow like water," depending on the intervals between the top and bottom tones.

This secret practice had seldom been performed in the West. Foreign to our musical languages, the tonal and timbral spectrum was chilling and inspiring. In the weeks that followed, the group sang in the Cathedral of St. John the Divine in New York and the Rothko Chapel in Houston.

Listening to these sounds for extended periods awakens us to the sonic spectrum. Distinguishing the subtle powers of tone is also easily developed by daily toning and by listening to recordings of fine overtone singers like the Gyuto and Gyume Tantric choirs or the solo singing of Michel Vetter. What seems like a magical feat of production becomes a natural extension of tonal power.

Lama Anagarika Govinda writes about these remarkable sounds in his book *The Way of the White Clouds:*

> Tibetan ritual music is not concerned with the emotions of temporal individuality, but with the ever-present, timeless qualities of universal life, in which our personal joys and sorrows do not exist. To bring us in touch with this realm is the purpose of meditation as well as of Tibetan ritual music, which is built upon the deepest vibrations that a human voice can produce: sounds that seem to come from the womb of the earth or from the depth of space like rolling thunder, the mantric sound of nature, which symbolizes the creative vibrations of the universe, the origin of all things.

These sounds in full array come not only from the throat, but also from the solar plexus, the base of the spine and the crown of the head. The whole body is a vibrating string and an air column at the same time.

People with clairvoyant sight tell of the dynamic contrast in colors that accompanies these sounds. The rituals are often called "transmissions" of the sacred teachings. The full body receives the text, the sonic power and the etheric message from a poignant, focused delivery.

This may be the highest achievement of harmonic singing and overtone control in the human voice. Today the popularity of the Tibetan styles and the Mongolian *hoomi* style overshadows the many other religious and ethnic traditions that integrate harmonic toning into their religious or shamanic practices.

These multiphonic sounds may seem gross and elemental to a Westerner with no experience of sophisticated tonal colors and textures. Yet this is the most refined and controlled integration of language, toning, and spiritual discipline I know. It is helpful to listen to these unique sounds for prolonged periods. We use many of these same powers in our speaking voice, but we move through them so quickly that we do not hear them unless we develop keen listening skills. We can experiment with our own voices to discover how these sonic secrets are concealed from our everyday vocal awareness.

Overtones are important in all choral singing. They are intuitively developed to blend different types of voices singing together. Barbershop quartets, Swiss yodelers and many Eastern European folk traditions mix harmonic colors to create unique blends of sound. The Scottish bagpipes and didjeridus of the Aborigines create harmonic effects without the clear, flute-effect of the Tibetans or Mongolians. The Yakuts, the Tuvins of the U.S.S.R., and the Gorno-Altai in Siberia all create amazing sounds high above a low drone.

Overtones exist in all vocal and instrumental sounds. Only the sine wave on an oscillator can produce a pure tone with no added colors or harmonics. Since the first harmonic above a fundamental sound is an octave higher than the original, we do not hear it as another note. The bass, root or fundamental note strongly resounds in the first, second, and third octave above itself. Other notes in the upper octave give the unique colors that allow us easily to identify the contrasting sounds of different instruments or voices.

What may seem like a nasal twang or swallowed sounds may be a highly controlled and sophisticated language, though foreign to us and perhaps not immediately grasped by our own sonic literacy. The meditation at the beginning of this chapter provides ample opportunity for you to become familiar with the harmonics in your own voice. If you repeat this exercise for a few days, you will come to hear the richness and interesting topography of the sounds in Tibetan singing.

Keyboard players are fated by the whims of the weather and the tempered (tampered) sounds that make the instrument seem in or out of tune, while string, wind, and brass players intuitively tune each note to the ensemble in which they are playing. Jazz musicians stretch the colors and the tones to brilliant extremes, while choral musicians use more conservative timbres to insure good vocal blend. What seems out of tune to the Western ear may be a delight to the ear of a Balinese or Chinese musician. I remember a Javanese friend asking me how I stayed charged and awake using only the simple sounds created on a keyboard.

Our sensitivity to sound has evolved with our music in the West. Each period of musical evolution has introduced new overtones. For the past fourteen centuries, the ways in which music would evolve have been predictable. According to master teacher Nadia Boulanger ("Lectures on Modern Music," Rice University Studies, 1925):

> "The dissonances of to-day are the consonances of tomorrow"—an immemorial commonplace of musical history which everyone knows in theory but whose force becomes apparent only by personal experience. To us it seems incredible that the interval of a third was once considered harsh or that Monteverdi (1568-1643) should have had difficulty in securing *droit de cité* for the chord of the dominant seventh.

Yet we all know that such was the case and that such will always be the fate of every new "dissonance".

The history of harmony is the history of the development of the human ear, which has gradually assimilated, in their natural order, the successive intervals of the harmonic series:

The platitudinous validity of the statement becomes obvious by comparison of the harmonic series with the following table, which gives—with only approximate accuracy—the chief diatonic chords in use during the successive periods of musical history.

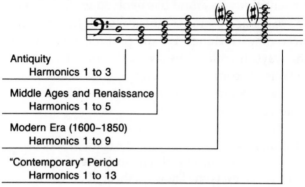

Antiquity
Harmonics 1 to 3

Middle Ages and Renaissance
Harmonics 1 to 5

Modern Era (1600–1850)
Harmonics 1 to 9

"Contemporary" Period
Harmonics 1 to 13

The early Gregorian scales, based on the sacred Greek modes, were notated in the sixth century. Their Greek names were kept, as were most of their sonic sequences. Dorian, Phrygian, Lydian, and Mixolydian were the most common modes. It was not until many centuries later that the Ionian mode came into popular use. It is known today as the major scale (the common Do, Re, Mi, Fa, Sol, La, Ti, Do progression). In India there are over 4,000 scales or *ragas*, each designated for a certain time of day, mood, or ritual. These are accompanied by *talas*, rhythmic modes that also have multipurpose emotional ranges.

Our Western modes slowly fell into disuse after the year 1600 when the didactic major scale (inappropriately labeled "happy" by music teachers) and minor scale (similarly misnamed "sad") became the usual standard for musical expression. We seemed to lose some of the range and subtlety of emotions available to the ancients by the very strange idea that there is "happy" music and "sad" music. Fortunately, through the educational innovation and intuitive awareness of Hungarian composer Zoltan Kodaly and German composer Carl Orff, American and British children are again being richly taught the pentatonic (five note) scales and ancient modes.

After centuries of unison singing in the Gregorian modes, the interval of the fifth was introduced in a style called Organum. Soon thereafter, intervals of fourths and thirds were used in melodic counterpoint to the old Gregorian melodies. As the centuries progressed, more chromatic music (half-steps, twelve tones per octave) introduced the intervals of seconds, using whole and half steps. Rules and laws about which notes could be sounded together developed. Compositions that broke these rules were considered diabolic and fictitious music. Those "evil" sounds of the fourteenth and sixteenth centuries are now quite acceptable to the liturgical ear, but Debussy and Ravel would have been burned in the Inquisition if they had been judged in that era by musical standards of the times.

It is of interest how our common scale—Do, Re, Mi, Fa, Sol, La, Si (modern Ti), Do—evolved. It was generally believed that sounds came down from heaven. Thus starting at the top of the scale:

Do	*Dominus*, God, Creator
Si (Ti)	Siderial, Stars, Galaxies, Cosmos
La	*Voie Lacte*, the Milky Way
Sol	*Sol*, the Sun
Fa	*Fatus*, Destiny, the Planets
Mi	Microcosmos, the Earth

| Re | *Regina Caeli,* Queen of Heaven, the Moon |
| Do | *Dominus,* God in Humanity |

Chinese, Indian, Balinese and numerous other musical systems have sacred strategies for the powers and evolution of tones as they are used harmonically. Quartertones and microtones are found in many traditions and have been coming into Western music for the last few decades.

With the introduction of electronic sounds, our tonal sensitivity is evolving. We are learning not to judge new sounds as evil and uncharged. We are living in a period where technology is creating new standards. As with all evolving forms of life, what is needed will be kept. What is of no use will atrophy. Truly, new spatial and ambient sounds are being produced that could not have been imagined at the turn of the century. It will take the masters of the age to perfect and explore these sounds with the dignity and ethics necessary for human development.

The great overtones yet to be discovered are those within the mind. The exploration we have yet to make is inward. Personally, I take a mesoteric view of the physical and spiritual development of humanity. Mesoteric philosophy is grounded in both the esoteric and the exoteric. It is the middle pillar view for the Kabbalist, the moderate stand, with full curiosity and respect for the diverse. It is an inclusive standpoint where diverse elements in a system can be equally honored without criticism. The tarot card *Temperance* exemplifies the balanced nature of standing within two worlds with dignity.

When I began exploring overtones in my own voice, my listening abilities changed. At the same time, my speaking voice became richer, fuller and healthier. I began working with students with reading disabilities, dyslexic tendencies, stuttering and physical handicaps. Suddenly, my knowledge of the ear and the brain clicked into place with what I knew of tone and breath. Great physical and emotional powers can become balanced and reemerge, much like Dr. Tomatis's description in the previous chapter. What at first seemed like regression in sound and music skills turned out to be just the opposite, the nurturing basics for development and superlative growth.

Each year I teach hundreds of classes and thousands of people in Asia, Africa, Europe and the Americas. Even if I cannot speak their language or model their social skills, I can sense and harmonize with the rhythmic expressions of the people. This is done both intuitively and in full consciousness. No matter how distant I may feel, working in a Black ghetto school in Chicago or on an elite cruise liner in the Mediterranean, I can harmonize and synchronize with greatly diverse rhythmic patterns. Whether I am in nursing homes, cancer wards, or schools systems with teachers who want to use music to teach reading, the rules are the same: Listen to the patterns. Listen to the rhythm of the emotion in the voices. Honor the place where the others are. Go out to them. Listen and guide them safely to new places of learning, well-being and balance. It is not always appropriate to make overtones, play Bach, or speak of esoteric things. But the breath and heartbeat are always there, ready to harmonize.

So far, I have refrained from mentioning my personal experiences of healing with tone. When one becomes familiar with tones through personal experiences and exercises, healing powers emerge. They are available to everyone with the right intention. It is appropriate to close this chapter with the most personal and significant experience with tone I have had in the past few years.

During my visit to Houston to hear the Gyuto Tantric Choir, I went to the home of my aunt. She had suffered a series of severe strokes over the previous two years. For months she had been motionless, speechless and unresponsive to outer stimulation. The psychological pressure on family and friends had been numbing.

The morning after I heard the monks sing, I visited her. It was a beautiful spring day. She lay in a bed near a window where she could see the tall pines. I had stayed in that room throughout my childhood and had fond, loving memories of my aunt taking me to Bible school and picnics. She had been a teacher and was greatly respected and loved. It was painful to see her lifeless, thin body working so hard to breathe.

Since I had planned to stay for a few hours, other family members left to do errands. I was left alone with my aunt. As on my other visits, I would tell her about my life, about the world she loved dearly and how much she was loved. I sang her favorite children's songs and hymns to her.

I had been experimenting with overtones. I realized that I could maintain a bass note and sing "Amazing Grace" in the higher harmonics, a couple of octaves higher than my regular singing voice. That hymn, as well as "Taps," "Reveille," and many pentatonic songs, were clearly constructed on the harmonic series, in the natural, sequential order. Knowing that no one else was around, I began to chant and tone "Amazing Grace" to her. I closed my eyes and imagined my aunt with a radiant golden light around her body, as if she were in the best of health. I sang and sang, repeating her treasured hymn in this strange way fifteen or twenty times. When I opened my eyes, her eyes were open too. I moved close to her and I thought I saw a smile. Then, from her right eye came a big tear.

I knew we had truly been together and both had understood the moment. I told her that everything was all right, that I knew she was well within, just weak in her body. I assured her everything was in order in her family, and I blessed her in my simple way. As I kissed her, my uncle returned. Another tear came from her right eye. I said good-bye.

My aunt died the next day.

Exercise: Making Overtones

Although it takes a while to develop the clear over-tones heard in Eastern chanting, it is not a completely foreign, mystical, and otherworldly art. We already produce overtones in our spoken vowel sounds.

This exercise will provide you with a few clues to discover how to make a double sound in your voice. It's like trying to learn to whistle. It seems impossible until somehow it happens. Then you can't really tell anyone else exactly how to do it.

You may wish to be alone when you try this exercise. Unsuspecting neighbors or family members may think you have become strange and otherworldly as you make these sounds.

Sit comfortably with your eyes closed. Shape your lips as though you had a straw in your mouth. Stretch your lower jaw downward. Imagine the inside of your mouth becoming a very large cave.

Yawn and hold your chin down with one hand as you begin to make a low "Ooo" sound. Remember to keep only a small opening in your lips. Then, gently and very gradually, without changing the pitch of the "Ooo," begin to change the sound to "You" and then to "Eee."

As you fully exhale with a small opening in your lips and your chin down, make a sound something like this:

"ooooooooooooouououououououuuuuuuuuuuuuu
eueueueueueeeeeeeeeeeeeee"

then

"eeeeeeeeeeeeeueueueueueuuuuuuuuuuuuuuuu
ououououououoooooooooooooooooo"

Do not be concerned about exactly how these vowel sounds are pronounced. If you begin with an "Oh" sound and move as slowly as possible to the "Eee" sound, you will naturally progress through all the other sounds. The key is to go very slowly and observe how your mouth and tongue change position as you modify the vowel sound ever so slightly.

Continue to go through this full sequence with each slow exhalation, with no break as you return to the darker sounding vowels. The slower you move your tongue between the vowel sounds, the more you will notice the overtones beginning to appear in your voice. This is not an authentic Tibetan technique, though it is somewhat similar to one of the Mongolian styles.

Making overtones is easier than you might suppose. Just start with these sounds, take your time, and know that you will discover a great power within your own voice. This exercise is very invigorating. But the greatest power of the tones occurs when the intention of the heart, the meaning of the sacred texts, and the vocal development are blended.

7
The Sound of Light

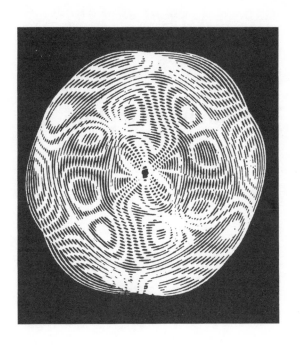

Meditation: The Ancient Future

Stand in a balanced, relaxed posture with your feet about eight inches apart. Turn your palms slightly to the front. Close your eyes. Allow each breath to balance and center your body.

As the potential of every plant and animal is held in its seed, so do the past and future coexist in each moment. Imagine the seed of all time, all creation, all being as present in your heart. With each inhalation, envision the wisdom, energy and heritage from the past as coming in through your feet up to your heart. When that image is clear, with each breath draw the wisdom, energy and potential from the future through your head and down to your heart.

Now, as you inhale, imagine bringing energies through your feet up to your heart. As you exhale, imagine the breath radiating out through your heart. On the next inhalation, bring the energies through your head down to your heart. Again, exhale through your heart. Keep repeating this sequence for several minutes. Let your breath fill the world around you with the sense of eternal Presence, the sacred NOW.

When your breathing and imaging become centered and relaxed, begin to tone the word "Home" so that it vibrates your chest and heart area. If you feel a little dizzy, sit down while you continue the meditation. But stand as much as possible.

"Home" is now. Here. Bonded. Harmonized. Free. "Home" is the Ancient Future, God's love. Now.

Key Words for Meditation: All is NOW.

The Sound of Light

The sound of light. The color of music. The touch of beauty. The power of love. The tone of creation. The vibration of life.

How difficult it is to unlock the feeling of these ideas with words. The left brain can hardly tolerate such immense intersensorial concepts. While they may seem nonlinear and practically impossible to grasp, another part of our mind distantly understands what the words represent. Douglas Anderson's book *The Planet of Waters* speaks of the great allegorical distance between thought, feeling, and language. Thinking of tone, of universal music, and of the inner powers of vibration takes the mind to a place of scientific, logical debate, a place of deep contemplation, or to a place of profound intuitive feeling. In Anderson's words:

Ours was the loveliest planet in the universe. We had always lived happily there. As far as we knew, that would never change.

Well, it did. The distance now is greater than I could count. If you built a ship to find where we came from, you might put your star-sailors into suspended animation. Or if you sent families, then perhaps the thousandth generation would see our first home. If they could.

But as you say, "You can't get there from here." We can't either. And by then, what would Earth be? Alive? Developed? Vanished from your mother galaxy? Broken to dust?

The cosmos is time's prison.

Besides, we did not come in starships. We came as ourselves on the currents. That was because of the music.

* * * * *

Rivers course through the oceans of Earth. You call them "streams" or "currents."

In just the same way, great streams of living music wander the universe. All the universe is an ocean of music. Your Plato guessed this when he named "the music of the spheres." You call music the universal language. It is also the universal bloodstream.

And that is how we came to be here—fugitives adrift on the current.

* * * * *

I will call our first home The Planet of Waters. But Oh to see it again, or if I could take you there.

Even now, when you are in a foreign country, and you try to tell someone of your feelings for your homeland, but you stumble over your own words, or even if you know the foreign language, it is hard to make the words express what you feel.

There was no land on The Planet of the Waters. A radiant, round core was at the center. The closer to the core, the cooler the waters, though not darker. The core sustained the planet; it pulsed with the living music, and it glowed.

And we lived there, in the waters; we breathed the waters, we loved there, we took bodies and made homes and communities.

In the still darkness of my aging heart, I can envision our whole world—radiant, lovely, slow—revolving through the warm black ocean. We were a layered Joseph's coat of round, fluid life, our many dyes of family zones gliding upon each other like hands pressing gently together but with no barriers like your skins, all within the ever-changing music of life itself.

* * * * *

We had two suns. The music of our planet's turning was in harmony with them, as Earth is with its one. There was light on the waters.

Sometimes there was light all the way around. Then, because of the swing of our orbits of the suns, The Planet of Waters passed between the suns. That happened every eight years (every one hundred twenty-eight by Earth time).

It was our season of creative magic. If we had used

123

words, we might have called it The Turn. For we could pass into or out of the seedcore of the planet.

In the waters we had bodies, and many different tribes. But inside the core we had no bodies.

At The Turn, those who chose to, passed into the core. Others came out, taking new bodies. There were always more wanting in than the core would take, and more wanting to rejoin the waters than the core would liberate.

This was a graceful exchange—like dancers changing places at a ball, except we changed not only place, but form. In the fine phrase of your master Shakespeare, we "suffered a sea change." And this was how our planet renewed itself.

When leaving the body to return to the seedcore, we surrendered everything except essence. Essence is music. Each of our souls is a tone, containing all the character of the individual. We were not "dead" while inside the seedcore, but alive and conscious.

This is difficult "to put your finger on," because you can't put a finger on it. Souls are invisible. Many "realities" are invisible: currents for example. Though you can't see a current, you know that when it ripples through water or wind, it can carry a raft across an ocean or wreck a city. Without current, the water and the wind would just lie there and do nothing.

You have an expression, "Seeing is believing." It is a good saying, though only for things which can be seen.

The greatest forces of creation are unseen. For example, love.

* * * * *

It is hard to sing our story: first because we, like you, have feelings. There are feelings through all the world.

Second, we have no language of words. We have tones. Our mind is like music. Even this name, "The Planet of Waters". . .I had to make it up. If I could simply sing you the name, you would already know it, "deja vu" become fact. My work here is not so much to "make words sing," but to make you a language from music.

Douglas Anderson,
The Planet of Waters

The prefrontal lobe of the brain has been called the "angel brain." Only here can we think about full systems. It is there that we experience empathy, justice, altruism, and spiritual love. To think of the powers of these states of mind, one must balance the body, enter the world of feeling, and then concentrate on the powers of thought. To harmonize these different states of mind and body is to attune them to each other, so that no one part of this symphonic self is dissonant.

How difficult it is to bring these states of being together. The left brain is always available to be critical, judgmental, and so rational that even the body cannot be heard. Yet the old memories and the eternal remembrances are also there, if only we allow the tuning to

125

take place. Spiritual experiences, moments of enlightenment, great pain and distress all take us away from the normal patterns of our daily lives. We long to raise our consciousness, our perception, and our experience. We wish to dissolve the disharmony.

To bring these rich and diverse contrasts into a vibrant, rich experience that includes the physical, emotional and mental is within the power of tone. Tone does not create more contrast in our lives; it expands harmony. The grand conductor of all systems and patterns is within us, capable of energizing and harmonizing all our powers of becoming.

If our brains were simple enough for us to understand them, we could not do so! Yet, there is something beyond the brain. It is the mind, the energy field of intelligence that is not confined in our simple, conscious thoughts. The force fields around our bodies carry the energies of our genetic history, no matter how many thousands of years old they may be. The energy fields around sacred sites, cities and continents pulse with the holorhythms of time. We still breathe a great portion of the same air as our ancient ancestors. We still walk on the same earth and swim in the same seas. Although polluted and often abused, the earth continues to hold the pulsing energy that sustains life.

Mother Earth holds us. She breathes, pulses, and tones at the low, inaudible 7.82 cycles per second during her daily and yearly rotation cycles. We all live in our own rhythms and tones and are affected by the rhythms and tones of others. And all life vibrates with its own harmonic relationship to earth. As we blend languages, peoples, attitudes and religions, we feel new harmonies emerge. We are challenged to find the common harmonies among thoughts and rhythms of life that seem foreign and at times alien. As we strive to create a peaceful world, we are challenged to know an energized peace which will allow movement through patterns in our shadows where we cannot see.

Music is energy. Music is metaphor. It is within sound and it is within silence. It is the rhythm of consciousness and it is the harmonics of life. As we continue to resolve the disharmonies in society, we cannot forget the great universe within. For it is here that mind, body and spirit will ultimately face the music. The eternal home that is heaven, earth, NOW and the future becomes one vibrating moment. Breath, tone and the attunement of all vibrations of the inner world and the outer will thus come into harmony. This is the mystery, the Roar of Silence.

Exercise: The Roar of Silence

Sit or stand in a balanced, comfortable position in a darkened room. Begin by closing your eyes and breathing deeply for two or three minutes, concentrating on the sound of your breath.

Then, on exhalation, begin to make sounds in the lowest part of your voice. You may form a growl or a low, purring sound. Do not force the voice, allow it to naturally and gradually begin to make these soft, rumbling sounds.

Then, add the word "Roooooooooooaaaaaaaaaaaaaar" to these low sounds. Notice all the different textures and overtones that you create as you gradually change the position of your tongue.

Spend three minutes making the sound. Notice the effects of the sound on your body. Then, without unnecessary left-brain thought, enter the silence again for three minutes, attending to your breathing.

Sound or breathe into any physical tension. Sound into random thoughts. Sound out emotions without words. Your voice is the intimate vessel of life force. Its vibrating power quickens you to an awakened life.

Bibliography

Anderson, Douglas. *The Planet of Waters*. Bread and Butter Press, 2582 S. Clayton, Denver, CO 80210, 1976.

Berendt, Joachim-Ernst. *Nada Brahma, The World is Sound*. Destiny Books, 1 Park Street, Rochester, VT 05767, 1987.

Campbell, Don G. *Introduction to the Musical Brain*. Magnamusic Baton, 10370 Page Industrial Blvd., St. Louis, MO 63132, 1983.

_____. *Master Teacher, Nadia Boulanger*. Pastoral Press, 225 Sheridan St. N.W., Washington, D.C. 20011, 1984.

Campbell, Jeremy. *Winston Churchill's Afternoon Nap*. Simon & Schuster, New York, 1986.

Cousto, Hans. *The Cosmic Octave: The Inherent Vibrations of Planets, Tones, Colors*. Life Octave Press, P.O. Box 806, Mendocino, CA 95460, 1988.

Crandall, Joanne. *Self-Transformation Through Music*. Theosophical Publishing House, Quest Books, Wheaton, IL, 1986.

Easwaran, Eknath. *The Mantram Handbook*. Nilgiri Press, Box 477, Petaluma, CA 94952, 1977.

Govinda, Lama Anagarika. *The Way of the White Clouds*. Rider and Co., London, 1966.

Gilmor, Madaule and Thompson, eds. *About the Tomatis Method*. Sound Listening Center, 2701 E. Camelback, Suite 205, Phoenix, AZ 85016, 1988.

Kahn, Hazrat Inayat. *The Music of Life*. Omega Press, 1570 Pacheco, Santa Fe, NM 87501, 1983.

Kayser, Hans. *Akroasis, The Theory of World Harmonics*. Plowshare Press, Box 2252, Boston, MA 02107, 1970.

Keyes, Laurel Elizabeth. *Toning, The Creative Power of the Voice*. DeVorss & Co., 1641 Lincoln Blvd., Santa Monica, CA 90404, 1973.

Leonard, George. *The Silent Pulse*. E. P. Dutton, New York, 1978.

Lewis, Robert C. *The Sacred Word and its Creative Overtones*. The Rosicrucian Press, Box 713, Oceanside, CA 92054, 1986.

Lingerman, Hal A. *The Healing Energies of Music*. Theosophical Publishing House, Quest Books, Wheaton, IL, 1983.

MacLean, Paul D. "Brain Evolution Relating to Family, Play, and the Separation Call." *Archives of General Psychiatry*, Volume 42. April, 1985.

McClellan, Randall. *The Healing Forces of Music*. Amity House, 18 High St., Warwick, NY 10990, 1988.

Reck, David. *Music of the Whole Earth*. Charles Scribner and Sons, New York, 1977.

Rudhyar, Dane. *The Magic of Tone and the Art of Music*. Shambhala, Boston, 1982.

_____. *Rhythm of Wholeness*. Theosophical Publishing House, Quest Books, Wheaton, IL, 1983.

Summer, Lisa. *Guided Imagery and Music*. Magnamusic Baton, 10370 Page Industrial Blvd., St. Louis, MO 63132, 1988.

Werbeck-Svardstrom, Valborg. *Uncovering the Voice*. Rudolph Steiner Press, London, 1980.

Wilson, Tim. "Chant, The Healing Power of Voice and Ear," documentary cassette on A. A. Tomatis. Institute for Music, Health and Education, Boulder, CO.

Yatri. *Unknown Man, The Mysterious Birth of a New Species*. Simon & Schuster, New York, 1988.

For an extended and thorough bibliography of resources on sound, please write to the Librarian, Institute for Music, Health and Education, P.O. Box 1244, Boulder, CO 80306.

Discography

The following records, tapes, and compact discs are suggested for use with the meditations and exercises. Each has a unique way of using elongated tones, repetitive patterns, and drones.

The Gyuto Tantric Choir. Tibetan Chanting. Windham Hill Records, Stanford, California.

Tantric Harmonics. The Gyume Tantric Choir. Spirit Music, Boulder, Colorado.

Angels. Don G. Campbell. Greater Spiral Records, Portland, Oregon.

Runes. Kano. Spirit Music, Boulder, Colorado.

Inward Harmony. Marcey Hamm. Harmony Records, Richardson, Texas.

Music for Airports, Ambient 1. Brian Eno. EG, Opal. Jem Records, Reseda, California.

Thursday Afternoon. Brian Eno. EG, Opal. Jem Records, Reseda, California.

Overtones. Michel Vetter. Harmonia Mundi, Los Angeles.

Vespers and Complines; Bishops and Doctors; Christmas, Easter. Gregorian Chant albums. The Monks of Solemnes, France. Paraclete Recordings, Orleans, Massachusetts.

About the Author

Don Campbell is composer, author, performer, teacher and consultant in psychoacoustics. He is Director of the Institute for Music, Health and Education in Boulder, Colorado and serves on the faculties of Naropa Institute and Boulder Graduate School, where he teaches classes in music, healing, and imagery.

Mr. Campbell is author of *Introduction to the Musical Brain* (Magnamusic, 1983) and *Master Teacher, Nadia Boulanger* (Pastoral Press, 1984). He is the composer/artist for the following albums: *Cosmic Classics, Crystal Meditations, Crystal Rainbows,* and *Runes* (Spirit Music, Boston/Boulder), *Lightning on the Moon* and *Angels* (Greater Spiral Records, Portland, Oregon), *Symphony For the Inner Self* (River Run Press, New York) and *Birthing* (Silverthread, Dallas). He is also composer of the ballets "Dances for a Sleepwalker" and "Like a Diamond in the Sky."

At age thirteen, Don Campbell became a student of Nadia Boulanger and Robert Casadesus at the Fontainebleau Conservatory of Music. He studied piano, harmony, and organ in France and Germany throughout his high school years.

For seven years, Mr. Campbell taught music and humanities at St. Mary's International School in Tokyo while serving as a music critic for an English newspaper. For four years he served as National Director of Education for the Choristers Guild, an international organization serving over 10,000 children's choirs.

Since 1982, Mr. Campbell has been a consultant in education and healing arts. He regularly teaches and lectures on the transformational uses of music throughout the United States, Europe, Africa, and Asia. He often keynotes conferences with innovative and creative presentations in the fields of accelerated memory, learning, and the uses of imagery in medicine and education.

Through a grant, the author researched the effects of music, listening, and improvisation on reading, dyslexia, and health. He was recently appointed to the Guggenheim Education Project in Chicago, which combines music, accelerated learning, and innovative curriculum for inner-city schools.

Mr. Campbell can be reached through the Institute for Music, Health, and Education, P.O. Box1244, Boulder, Colorado, 80306.